# *Still Dews*

***

*Other anthologies compiled by Fiona Castle*

LET ME COUNT THE WAYS
RAINBOWS THROUGH THE RAIN
WHAT A WONDERFUL WORLD

*

*Also by Fiona Castle*

CANCER'S A WORD, NOT A SENTENCE

# *Still Dews*

***

## AN ANTHOLOGY OF PEACE

## Fiona Castle

Hodder & Stoughton
LONDON  SYDNEY  AUCKLAND

British Library Cataloguing in Publication Data
A record for this book is available from
the British Library

ISBN  0 340 78677 9

Printed and bound in Great Britain
by Clays Ltd, St Ives plc

Hodder and Stoughton
A division of Hodder Headline Ltd
338 Euston Road
London NW1 3BH

# Dedication

***

Since the compiling of this book we have witnessed the devastation of the World Trade Center in New York and have wept and prayed for those who have experienced the death of loved ones as a result.

I was moved by a comment made by President George W. Bush. He said that every person who had died in the tragedy was the most important person in the world to somebody.

It is to that precious 'somebody' that I dedicate this book.

# Contents

✳ ✳ ✳

# *Acknowledgments*

✳ ✳ ✳

While every effort has been made to contact the copyright holders of material used in this book, this has not always been successful. Full acknowledgment will gladly be made in future editions.

We gratefully acknowledge the following:

Johann Christoph Arnold, extract from *Seeking Peace* (Plough Publishing House, 1998), used with permssion.

Eddie Askew, extract from *Slower than Butterflies*, published by The Leprosy Mission International and used with permission.

Gordon Bailey, extract from *Mix and Match* (Schools Outreach, 1999), used by kind permission of the author.

Alistair Begg, extract from *The Hand of God*, Moody Press, copyright 1999. Used with permission

Harry Boyle, 'Peace' and 'Serenity', used by kind permission of the author.

Extract from T. S. Eliot, *Murder in the Cathedral*, Faber and Faber. Used with permission.

Bob Gass, extracts from *The Word for Today*, published by United Christian Broadcasters and used by permission. For free copies of the quaterly devotional, contact UCB, PO Box 255, Stoke-on-Trent ST4 8YY.

Living Light © 1972 by Tyndale House Publishers, Inc., Wheaton, IL USA. All rights reserved.

*Living Light: Selections from the Living Bible*, Kingsway, 1976. Used by permission of Kingsway Publications, Lottbridge Drove, Eastbourne.

Walter de la Mare, 'The Linnet', 'Nod' and 'Silver', used with permission of the Literary Trustees of Walter de la Mare and the Society of Authors as their representative.

Scripture quotations marked (NLT) are taken from the Holy Bible, *New-wing Translation*, copyright © 1996. Used by permission of Tyndale House Publishers, Inc., Wheaton, IL USA. All rights reserved.

Lloyd Ogilvie, extracts from *Turn Your Struggles Into Stepping Stones* and *Let God Love You* by permission of W Publishing Group.

Aub Podlich, extract from *Beyond the Trees*, copyright Openbook Publishers (formerly Lutheran Publishing House). Used with permission.

Noel Richards, 'To Be in Your Presence', copyright © 1991 Kingsway's Thankyou Music, PO Box 75, Eastbourne, East Sussex BN23 6NW, UK. tym@kingsway.co.uk. Used by permission.

*The Soldier's Armoury*, used by permission of The Salvation Army.

Ian Smale, 'Angels', copyright © 1988 Kingsway's Thankyou Music, PO Box 75, Eastbourne, East Sussex BN23 6NW, UK. tym@kingsway.co.uk. Used by permission.

# CHAPTER ONE

# Dear Lord and father of mankind, forgive our foolish ways

\* \* \*

Dear Lord and Father of mankind
Forgive our foolish ways!
Reclothe us in our rightful mind,
In purer lives thy service find,
In deeper reverence, praise.

In simple trust like theirs who heard,
Beside the Syrian sea,
The gracious calling of the Lord,
Let us, like them, without a word,
Rise up and follow thee.

O Sabbath rest by Galilee!
O calm of hills above,
Where Jesus knelt to share with thee
The silence of eternity,
Interpreted by love!

Drop thy still dews of quietness,
Till all our strivings cease,
Take from our souls the strain and stress,
And let our ordered lives confess
The beauty of thy peace.

Breathe through the heats of our desire
Thy coolness and thy balm;
Let sense be dumb, let flesh retire;
Speak through the earthquake, wind and fire,
O still small voice of calm!

*J. G. Whittier*

*The writer of this wonderfully descriptive hymn, J. G. Whittier, was an American Quaker who, through his love of the written word and of poetry in particular, became editor of a Philadelphia newspaper, the* Pennsylvania Freeman. *He used this position to work for social justice, including the abolition of slavery. As a result, his own life was anything but 'peaceful', as this hymn intimates. However, the underlying meaning of the words of these verses shows us that real peace is found, not in the absence of activity or strife, but through our spiritual relationship with God, our Creator. The price was the death on the cross of his own Son, Jesus Christ.*

*For this reason, the words of the first verse of the hymn are so significant: 'Forgive our foolish ways'. To acknowledge our guilt and to ask for forgiveness is the only way to mend any relationship; never more so than with God.*

Finally, I confessed all my sins to you
   and stopped trying to hide them.
I said to myself 'I will confess my rebellion
   to the LORD.'
   And you forgave me! All my guilt is gone.

*Psalm 32:5 (NLT)*

## FORGIVENESS: THE KEY TO REAL PEACE

When people say they have no need of God
they usually mean that they are quite happy
without God. What they fail to realise is that
our greatest need is not 'happiness' but
'forgiveness'.

We all need forgiveness. Without it we are
in serious trouble. For God is not only our
loving Father; He is also a righteous judge.

*Nicky Gumbel, from* Why Jesus?

Imprisoned one,
Caught up in
Fears and failures,
Hopelessly ensnared,
Try to remember ...

Discouraged one,
Entangled in life's
Pain and problems,
Thinking no one cares,
Try to remember ...

When you can't find the way,
You need to find The Way,
Jesus is still
The Way,
The Truth,
The Life.
He was your Way in,
And He is your Way out.

Escape into His freedom.
Do this in remembrance of Him.

*Susan Lenzkes*

Jesus Christ's claim is that He can put a new disposition, His own disposition, Holy Spirit, into any man, and it will be manifested in all that he does. But the disposition of the Son of God can only enter my life by the way of repentance.

*Oswald Chambers*

Peace, perfect peace, in this dark world of sin? The blood of Jesus whispers peace within.

*Edward Henry Bickersteth,* Songs in the House of Pilgrimage

We need the peace of Christ especially in times of failure. In every human failure there are three elements: what happened, and how we react to what happened, and what we allow Christ to give us to change our reaction to what happened. Usually we brood over the failure in our own strength. That almost always leads to remorse and to justifying ourselves by explaining it away or by blaming someone else or some other circumstances. On the other hand, the peace Christ offers is radically different. It is the peace that floods our hearts when we honestly acknowledge whatever part we've had in the failure. When we experience Christ's forgiveness, we can forgive ourselves. Out of that comes the freedom to forgive the people who may have caused the failure. Being a Christian doesn't mean we always have to take the blame, but it does mean that we must forgive. The sooner the better.

Failures bring us back to the death and the resurrection experience of profound peace. When we fail or must forgive someone whose failure has caused us pain, eventually we have to admit we can't handle it ourselves. That shatters our false pride. In a mysterious way that wilful person inside us has to die so that the new person Christ wants to make us can live. I think that's a vital part of what it means to take up our cross. Our pride is crucified, we die to our own pride, and out of the ashes of whatever the failure was, we are raised up to a new beginning to live with the calm confidence of Christ's peace and the fear-dispelling strength of His courage. Then we can say with Paul, 'I have been crucified with Christ; it is no longer I who live, but Christ lives in me; and the life which I now live in the flesh I live by faith in the Son of God, who loved me and gave himself for me' (Galatians 2:20).

*J. Lloyd Ogilvie, from* Turn your Struggles into Stepping Stones

God exhausts metaphors to show what His forgiveness means – 'I, even I, am He that blotteth out thy transgressions for Mine own sake, and will not remember thy sins'; 'I have blotted out, as a thick cloud, thy transgressions, and as a cloud, thy sins'; 'As far as the east is from the west, so far hath He removed our transgressions from us'; 'For Thou hast cast all my sins behind Thy back'; 'For I will forgive their iniquity, and I will remember their sin no more.'

When we turn to God and say we are sorry, Jesus Christ has pledged His word that we will be forgiven, but the forgiveness is not operative unless we turn, because our turning is the proof that we know we need forgiveness.

*Oswald Chambers*

*You cannot repent too soon, for you do not know how soon it will be too late!*

'If my people who are called by my name will humble themselves and pray and seek my face and turn from their wicked ways, I will hear them from heaven and will forgive their sins and heal their land.'

*2 Chronicles 7:14 (NLT)*

## INNER PEACE

Peace I leave with you, my peace I give unto you: not as the world giveth, give I unto you. Let not your heart be troubled, neither let it be afraid.

*John 14:27 (AV)*

'Thou will keep him in perfect peace, whose mind is stayed on thee, because he trusteth in thee.' (Isaiah 26:3, AV)

The peace of God is not the peace of stoicism or passivity. It is the most intense activity. Some people say that they are tired of life; they mean to say that they are tired of dying. They are tired of the spiritual death that stops activity. They are tired of life getting so sluggish.

What does Jesus say? 'I have come that ye might have life and that ye may have it more abundantly; but ye will not come to me that ye might have it.' Everything in this natural world is pitted against you and unless you have His life you will never have real peace.

*Oswald Chambers*

*T*he most wonderful day of my life was the day I discovered the truth of the Bible verse above. It was a time in my life when I had everything but peace. I had all the material comfort I needed, but I *was stressed out and miserable. I talked to a friend, tearfully, about all my troubles and she gently showed me that it was possible to live a different way, by letting go of the failure I had made of my life, asking God to forgive me and inviting Jesus to take over whatever remained of my life.*

*I didn't believe at that time that anything would make any difference to my life, but I was suddenly overwhelmed by peace! It poured all over me like soothing balm, releasing all the tension in my life.*

*That was the brand new start God gave me in 1975 and since then I have proved that his peace is not based on circumstances, so it doesn't disappear when life gets tough!*

To find your peace take the journey from the head to the heart.

*Anon.*

I never knew up to that time that God loved us so much. This heart of mine began to thaw out; I could not keep back the tears. I just drank it in ... I tell you there is one thing that draws above everything else in the world, and that is love.

*D. L. Moody*

Now think for a moment about the meaning of this word 'peace'. Does it seem strange to you that the angels should have announced Peace, when ceaselessly the world has been stricken with War and the fear of War? Does it seem to you that the angelic voices were mistaken, and that the promise was a disappointment and a cheat?

Reflect now, how Our Lord Himself spoke of Peace. He said to His disciples, 'Peace I leave with you, my peace I give unto you.' Did He mean peace as we think of it: the kingdom of England at peace with its neighbours, the barons at peace with the King, the householder counting over his peaceful gains, the swept hearth, his best wine for a friend at the table, his wife singing to the children? Those men His disciples knew no such things: they went forth to journey afar, to suffer by land and sea, to know torture, imprisonment, disappointment, to suffer death by martyrdom. What then did He mean? If you ask that, remember then that He said also, 'Not as the world gives, give I unto you.' So then, He gave to His disciples peace, but not peace as the world gives.

*T. S. Eliot, from* Murder in the Cathedral


In His will is our peace.

*Dante*

Those who live as if there is no afterlife will gain nothing if they are proved to be right, and will lose everything if they are proved to be wrong. Those who live as though the present influences the next world have lost nothing if they are proved to be wrong, and will have gained everything if they are proved to be right.

*Blaise Pascal*

## BROKEN CISTERNS THAT CAN'T HOLD WATER!

The people who lived there began to talk about building a great city, with a temple-tower reaching to the skies – a proud, eternal monument to themselves. God scattered them all over the earth; and that ended the building of the city. I worked hard to be wise instead of foolish – but now I realise that even this was like chasing the wind. For the greater my wisdom, the greater my grief; to increase knowledge only increases distress. Then I tried to find fulfilment by inaugurating a great public works programme; homes: vineyards: gardens: parks and orchards for myself, and reservoirs to hold the water to irrigate my plantations. I collected silver and gold as taxes from many kings and provinces. But as I looked at everything I had tried, it was all so useless, a chasing of the wind, and there was nothing really worthwhile anywhere.

If anyone is thirsty, let him come to me and drink. For he satisfies the thirsty soul and fills the hungry soul with good.

Let heaven fill your thoughts; don't spend your time worrying about things down here.

*From* Living Light

## HE IS OUR PEACE

Not in the absence of strife
But in the midst of life
Do we encounter peace –
Here, in the breaking of bread
In the precious blood He shed
Do we find peace.
This Man of Sorrows
Who stilled the raging of the sea,
He is our peace.
Who made the lame to walk
And set the prisoner free,
Who after conquering death
And with renewing breath
Spoke 'peace' to each
And every friend,
Has promised to be with us to the end
This man of gentleness

This King of love
Has given the Holy Spirit from above,
Jesus' rule and reign shall never cease,
He is our Lord, our life,
Our Prince of Peace.

*Marilyn Dougan,* a dear friend

*O*ne of the best definitions of peace I have read comes from Phillip Keller in his book, A Gardener Looks at the Fruits of the Spirit:

Peace is the selfless, self-giving, self-losing, self forgetting, self sacrificing love of God in repose despite all the adverse reverses of life. It is love standing serene, strong, and stable in spite of every insult, every antagonism, every hate.

Peace is the spirit and soul of persons so imbued with the presence of God's Gracious Spirit that they are not easily provoked. They are not 'touchy'. They are not irritable or easily enraged. Their pride is not readily pricked. They do not live like a bristling porcupine with all its quills extended in agitated self-defence.

Peace is actually the exact opposite. It is the quiet, potent, gracious attitude or serenity and good-will that comes to meet the onslaught of others with good cheer, equanimity, and strong repose.

To see and understand this quality of life at its best we simply must turn away from our contemporaries and look at Christ … God very God …

He is known as the God of all peace. He alone is the source and supplier of peace. Active in our attitudes and actions, He alone can produce this quality of life in our everyday experiences.

All through human history God has approached men in peace. Always He has come amongst us with good will. This was dramatised in the incredible declaration of the angels on the night of His advent: 'On earth, peace good will toward men' (Luke 2:14).

This has ever been God's generous, magnanimous approach to humanity, despite man's most despicable hatred and opposition to His overtures of good will. It matters not where God's Spirit finds a man or woman, His approach is always in peace. It matters not how deep the sin, how dark the stain, how set the soul in selfishness – Christ comes to us in peace.

He has our redemption in view and our ultimate renewal in mind. He has our restoration to His family as the supreme goal of His own goodness. He comes to us with arms outstretched with brimming eyes that have looked upon us with longing, with His Spirit spilling over with goodwill.

*W. Phillip Keller*

A great many people are trying to make peace, but that has already been done. God has not left it for us to do; all we have to do is enter into it.

*D. L. Moody*

The time of business does not differ with me from the time of prayer ... In the noise and clutter of my kitchen, while several persons at the same time are calling different things, I possess God in as great tranquillity as if I were upon my knees.

*Brother Lawrence*

Like a river glorious is God's perfect peace,
Over all victorious, in its bright increase:
Perfect yet it floweth, fuller every day;
Perfect yet it groweth deeper all the way.
*Stayed upon Jehovah, hearts are fully blest;*
*Finding, as He promised, perfect peace and rest.*

Hidden in the hollow of His blessed hand,
Never foe can follow, never traitor stand;
Not a surge of worry, not a shade of care,
Not a blast of hurry touch the spirit there.
*Stayed upon Jehovah, hearts are fully blest;*
*Finding, as He promised, perfect peace and rest.*

*Frances R. Havergal*

## PEACE IS JOY RESTING

The peace of God, which passeth all understanding, shall keep your hearts and minds through Christ Jesus.

*Philippians 4:7 (AV)*

Let the peace of God rule in your hearts.

*Colossians 3:15 (AV)*

'These things write we unto you, that your joy may be full.' What is fullness of joy but peace? Joy is tumultuous only when it is not full; but peace is the privilege of those who are 'filled with the knowledge of the glory of the Lord, as the waters cover the sea'. 'Thou wilt keep him in perfect peace, whose mind is stayed in Thee, because he trusteth in Thee.' It is peace, springing from trust and innocence, and then overflowing in love towards all around him. He who is anxious, thinks of himself, is suspicious of danger, speaks hurriedly, and has no time for the interests of others; he who lives in peace is at leisure, wherever his lot is cast.

*John Henry Newman*

# CHAPTER TWO

# *Reclothe us in our rightful mind*

\* \* \*

When we discover the reality of God's peace, He changes our minds, our attitudes and helps us to see life from His point of view. Then we begin to see the folly of all the hindrances to His peace ... class and racial discrimination, anger, pride and greed ... He gives us a social conscience and a desire to make a difference.

Peace and prosperity, tranquillity and security are only possible if these are enjoyed by all without discrimination.

*Nelson Mandela*

Everybody can be great. Because anybody can serve. You don't have to have a college degree to serve. You don't have to make your subject and your verb agree to serve. You don't have to know Einstein's Theory of Relativity to serve. You don't have to know the second theorem of thermo-dynamics in physics to serve. You only need a heart full of grace. A soul generated by love.

*Martin Luther King*

## PRAYER FOR PEACE

O God, whose will is life and peace
For all the sons of men,
Let not our human hates release
The sword's dread power again.
Forgive our narrowness of mind;
Destroy false pride, we plead:
Deliver us and all mankind
From selfishness and greed.

O God, whose ways shall lead to peace,
Enlighten us, we pray;
Dispel our darkness and increase
The light along our way.
Illumine those who lead the lands
That they may make at length
The laws of right to guide the hands
That wield the nations' strength.

O God, who callest us to peace,
We join with everyone
Who does his part that wars may cease
And justice may be done.
Enable us to take the way
The Prince of Peace hath trod;
Create the will to build each day
The family of God.

*Rolland W. Schloerb*

Pride is like a cancer of the soul. Beginning with a few cells of self-congratulation, boasting, or vanity, it soon grows unchecked into arrogance and conceit. Soon there is no room left for the healthy cells that worship God and pursue healthy purposes. As with cancer, the key to eliminating pride is to subject it to the surgeon's scalpel before it has a chance to grow out of control. Through confession and repentance, invite God to cleanse your heart of pride.

*Touchpoint – New Living Translation Bible*

*I have learnt, as a Christian, that I have to be willing to stand up and be counted; to stick my head above the parapet, when I know I will be shot; to speak out against injustice, lies and compromise. If it is hard, it is much harder to live with myself when I sit back and do nothing.*

## FALSE PEACE

We have our peace movements, and all we want is peace – abroad and at home. But if by peace we mean appeasing tyranny, compromising with gangsters and being silent because we haven't the moral fortitude to speak out against injustice, then this is not real peace. It is a false peace. It is a farce and it is a hoax.

*Billy Graham*


This above all: to thine own self be true,
And it must follow, as the night the day,
Thou canst not then be false to any man.

*William Shakespeare*

But Moses told the people, 'Don't be afraid, just stand where you are and watch the LORD rescue you ... The LORD himself will fight for you. You won't have to lift a finger in your defence!'

*Exodus 14:13–14 (NLT)*


Some say that the age of chivalry is past. The age of chivalry is never past, so long as there is a wrong left unredressed on earth, or a man or woman left to say, 'I will redress that wrong, or spend my life in the attempt.' The age of chivalry is never past, so long as we have faith enough to say, 'God will help me to redress that wrong; or if not me, he will help those that come after me, for His eternal Will is to overcome evil with good.'

*Charles Kingsley*


Proud and wicked people viciously oppress the poor.

*Psalm 10:2 (NLT)*

In the end, the cries of the infant who dies because of hunger, or because a machete has slit open his stomach, will penetrate the noises of the modern city and its sealed windows to say: I am human too.

*Nelson Mandela*

They create desolation and call it peace.

*Tacitus*

I wanted South Africa to see that I loved even my enemies, while I hated the system that turned us against one another.

*Nelson Mandela*

Once, while we were on roll call, a cruel guard kept us standing for a long, long time. Suddenly a skylark began to sing in the sky, and all the prisoners looked up to listen to that bird's song. As I looked at the bird I saw in the sky, I thought of Psalm 103:11. O Love of God, how deep and great; far deeper than man's deepest hate. God sent that skylark daily for three weeks, exactly during roll call, to turn our eyes away from the cruelty of men to the ocean of His love.

*Corrie ten Boom*

Two men looked out through prison bars,
The one saw mud; the other, stars.

*Anon.*

Lord, make me an instrument of thy peace.

*St Francis of Assisi*

Most of us have lost any clear sense of our
species' place in global ecosystems, and of our
biological kinship with other living things.

*David Suzuki*

## A SENSE OF PLACE

Somehow, in all this inner turmoil, you must
find your place. You do have a place. The
key to finding it is in the world of the Spirit.
If you do not find your place, you will never
really know how to live on this earth.

And that can be disastrous, not only for the
person involved, but for the earth as well –
as you can see by observing those who have
never found their place here, or have even
considered that they might have lost it.
Nothing good comes of losing your place in
the family of all things!

David Suzuki informs us brilliantly from his viewpoint as a humanist and scientist. He observes things as a biologist. He sees people over-tinkering with the building blocks of the world; forgetting our place in the family of all things, we have already started to pull the whole house down around our ears.

To a scientist, this is a crime against nature. Christians, and especially those who are scientists, consider this a rebellion against God. We Christians, too, believe in a family of all things. The more we are informed by the various scientific disciplines, the more we stand in awe at the interwoven web of all created things. 'What pattern connects the crab to the lobster and the orchid to the primrose, and all four of them to me and me to you?' asks Gregory Bateson. The science of ecology is the study of God's household, of relationship, of connectedness between all things.

For us who live knowingly within the arms of one great Father, who is the Person of Love behind everything, the connection between all things on earth goes far beyond what is biological. We are one with the animals, birds, and earth. This is the point, in Genesis, of our common origin from the earth. In family with the birds and animals, we are also creatures lovingly fashioned by holy hands, with the Father's own breath breathed into us.

Moreover, all creation came into being through a powerful word – a word spoken by no human being, animal, or planet. That same Word, having spoken, became for a time a human being who walked on this created earth; even now 'in him all things hold together' (Colossians 1:17, NIV), and he 'sustain(s) the universe with his powerful word' (Hebrews 1:3, GNB). That great living Word of God is the Man Jesus Christ. In some mysterious way, which I cannot even begin to understand, he connects me, through his own body, to every creature that exists in the universe.

The whole wide family of creation is therefore holy. Shaped lovingly by the fingers of God, breathed on, spoken into being, once visited and now held together by Jesus, this whole earth-family of mine is embraced by holy arms. Sacred place? It is all sacred place! It is his place.

In his place, I have been given a special place of my own. If I were to burst arrogantly out of my place, so that I begin to threaten the place of other living things, then I must answer to him. On the other hand, the more I search his mind, the more I see my place as assisting every other created being to live freely in its place.

*Aub Podlich, from* Beyond the Trees

Give us, Lord God, a vision of our world as your
   love would make it:
A world where the weak are protected, and none
   go hungry or poor;
A world where the benefits of civilised life are
   shared, and everyone can enjoy them;
A world where different races, nations and cultures
   live in tolerance and mutual respect;
A world where peace is built with justice, and
   justice is guided by love;
And give us the inspiration and courage to build
   it, through Jesus Christ our Lord, Amen.

*The Revd Trevor Williams, Leader of the Corrymeela
Community, an ecumenical community of
reconciliation in Northern Ireland*

There are no quick fixes in the work of
Reconciliation, it is a web of right relationships. One break destroys the whole. To
work for peace you need a clear vision to
maintain your energy and nourish your hope.
The love of God alone brings this about.

*The Revd Trevor Williams*

From the prison of anxious thought that
    greed has builded,
From the fetters that envy has wrought, and
    pride has gilded,
From the noise of the crowded ways and
    the fierce confusion,
From the folly that wastes its days in a
    world of illusion,
(Ah, but the life is lost that frets and
    languishes there!)
I would escape and be free in the joy of the
    open air.

By the faith that the flowers show when
    they bloom unbidden,
By the calm of the river's flow to a goal that
    is hidden,
By the trust of the tree that clings to its
    deep foundations,
By the courage of wild birds' wings on the
    long migration,
(Wonderful secret of peace that abides in
    Nature's breast!)
Teach me how to confide, and live my life,
    and rest.

*H. van Dyke*

I have held many things in my hands and I have lost them all; but whatever I have placed in God's hands, that I still possess.

*Martin Luther*

He is no fool who gives what he cannot keep to gain what he cannot lose.

*Jim Elliot*

You thought you were indifferent to praise for achievements which you would not yourself have accounted to your credit, or that, if you should be tempted to feel flattered, you would always remember that the praise far exceeded what the events justified. You thought yourself indifferent – until you felt jealousy flare up at someone else's naïve attempts to 'make himself important,' and your self-conceit stood exposed.

Concerning the hardness of the heart and its littleness, let me read with open eyes the book my days are writing – and learn.

*Dag Hammarskjöld*

In peace there's nothing so becomes a man
As modest stillness and humility.

*William Shakespeare*

## THE ABUNDANT LIFE

We will never arrive at a perfect state of
peace. Or find it once and for all. We can
follow the stepping stones across the water
as cautiously and earnestly as we like, but on
the other side we will still be ourselves.

All the same, there is no question that
once we experience peace, our hearts are
opened to a new dimension of living. In a
sense, that new dimension is much more
than a matter of peace. It is the new
existence promised us by Jesus when He
said, 'I have come to bring you life, that you
may have it abundantly.'

*Johann C. Arnold, from* Seeking Peace

## DEALING WITH OUR DARK SIDE

The house of the inner self is not always a place of peace. It can also be a place of turmoil and struggle. One of the things with which we constantly grapple is how to sustain our resolve to do what is right. We are all aware of forces within us which pull us away from the good. And within ourselves we can nurture desires which ultimately will be destructive.

[Henri] Nouwen reminds us that 'what remains hidden, kept in the dark, incommunicable can easily become a destructive force always ready to explode in unexpected moments.' What is kept in the dark ultimately becomes the dark side of ourselves. What is indulgently nurtured in our inner thoughts finally becomes part of our being.

While with great effort we may be able to bring these unwholesome thoughts under control, we frequently need to walk the road of humility by opening this part of our life to another person. We then need the help of a trusted friend who cares for us in ways that go deeper than our public persona. This friend must be able to hear the story of our turmoil and extend to us grace, forgiveness and peace.

*Charles Ringma, from* Dare to Journey
with Henry Nouwen

We are either 'pilgrims' or 'planners.' 'Planners' spend their time trying to match up and fit into their lifestyle and priorities set by others, and measure the value of their social achievements in terms of material success. 'Pilgrims' on the other hand cope with the unpredictability of life, accept human vulnerability and see life's ups and downs in terms of opportunities for human growth.

*Norman Shanks*


## SUCCESS

[On Mark 4:19] When we turn our eyes from the Lord to worldly attractions, we divert not only our eyes but our energy. Our lust, pride, and desire for possessions will smother our spiritual success and other areas of achievement as well. The best way to keep other things from crowding out God's Word is to keep God's Word regularly before us.

*Touchpoint – New Living Translation Bible*

43

But all too quickly the message is crowded out by the cares of this life, the lure of wealth, and the desire for nice things ...

*Jesus, telling parable of the sower*
*– Mark 4:19 (NLT)*

I worked hard to be wise instead of foolish – but now I realise that even this was like chasing the wind. For the greater my wisdom, the greater my grief; to increase knowledge only increases distress. Then I tried to find fulfilment by inaugurating a great public works programme: homes, vineyards, gardens, parks and orchards for myself, and reservoirs to hold the water to irrigate my plantations. I collected silver and gold as taxes from many kings and provinces. But as I looked at everything I had tried, it was all so useless, a chasing of the wind, and there was nothing really worthwhile anywhere.

*Taken from Ecclesiastes 1 and 2 (Living Bible)*

## THE WORLD IS TOO MUCH WITH US

The world is too much with us; late and soon,
Getting and spending, we lay waste our powers;
Little we see in nature that is ours;
We have given our hearts away, a sordid boon!
This sea that bares her bosom to the moon;
The winds that will be howling all the hours
And are up-gathered like sleeping flowers;
For this, for everything, we are out of tune;
It moves us not – Great God! I'd rather be
A Pagan suckled in a creed outworn;
So might I, standing on this pleasant lea,
Have glimpses that would make me less forlorn;
Have sight of Proteus rising from the sea;
Or hear old Triton blow his wreathèd horn.

*William Wordsworth*

## IF ONLY

If only he'd faced up to life as life is,
Instead of inventing the lies;
If only he hadn't believed his own dreams,
If only he'd not fantacised;
If only he'd seen where his folly might lead,
If only he'd lifted the lid;
But he closed his mind to the truth he might find;
If only he'd not – but he did.

If only she'd questioned his motives that night,
If only she'd looked past his smile;
If only she'd dwelt on that glimmer of doubt,
If only she'd paused for a while;
If only she hadn't suppressed common-sense
When the eager young man made his bid,
She wouldn't be racked with grief and despair;
If only she'd not – but she did.

If only I hadn't have tried to assess
What I might achieve in return;
If only I'd offered myself to them both,
If only I'd showed some concern;
If only I'd not closed my eyes to their needs,
If I hadn't scamped and hid,
When I could have been of some help to my friends;
If only I'd not – but I did!

*Gordon Bailey, from* Mix and Match

People who breezily testify to having not a
care in the world may deserve, not our envy,
but our pity. There is a peace – if it can be
called that – which may be possessed by a
man who has never faced a real problem, and
who has never seen – or if he has seen, never
felt – the agony of a pain-filled bed or the
heartbreak of a tender relationship that has
turned sour.

There is a kind of peace that may come to the unimaginative and insensitive, who shuts his eyes to human need. But this is not the peace of which the New Testament speaks. This operates in the midst of life's pains and perplexities. It depends on faith, or trustful commitment, which involves, of course, submission to God's will – obedience, as we have already seen. No one can expect to enjoy the peace of God who is unwilling to follow the way of God.

In a little book, *The Verdict of Experience*, Howard Stanley writes on this theme, and quotes the words of a distinguished Quaker, which, he says, have helped him. 'If you take a few steps along a road and discover as you go that your mind is uneasy and your heart disturbed, turn back. This is not the way for you. But if, on the other hand, you are travelling a road which is hard to the feet, which tests your strength and endurance, but you find that you are happy and assured, then continue along that road, for it is the way of God's choosing. The peace of God and the will of God go hand in hand.'

*from* The Soldiers Armoury, *14 June 1973*

*This is a prayer that I took very seriously after it was said at my 'confirmation' service at twelve years old:*

> Go forth into the world in peace;
> Be of good courage;
> Hold fast that which is good;
> Render to no man evil for evil;
> Strengthen the faint-hearted;
> Support the weak; help the afflicted;
> Honour all men; love and serve the Lord;
> Rejoicing in the power of the Holy Spirit;
> And the blessing of God Almighty,
> The Father, the Son and the Holy Ghost be
>     upon you
> And remain with you forever.

The LORD gives his people strength. The LORD blesses them with peace.

*Psalm 29:11 (NLT)*

# CHAPTER THREE

# *In purer lives thy service find*

\* \* \*

Resign every forbidden joy; restrain every
wish that is not referred to His will; banish
all eager desires, all anxiety. Desire only the
will of God; seek Him alone, and you will
find peace.

*Fénelon*

The question of where to live and what to do is really insignificant compared to the question of how to keep the eyes of my heart focussed on God. I can be teaching at Yale, working in the bakery at the Genesee Abbey, or walking around with poor children in Peru, and feel totally useless, miserable, and depressed in all these situations.

There is no such thing as the right place, the right job, the right calling or ministry. I can be happy or unhappy in all situations. I am sure of it because I have been. I have felt distraught and joyful in situations of abundance as well as poverty, in situations of popularity and anonymity, in situations of success and failure. The difference was never based on the situation itself, but always on my state of mind and heart. When I knew I was walking with God, I always felt happy and at peace. When I was entangled in my own complaints and emotional needs, I always felt restless and divided.

It is a simple truth that comes to me now, in a time when I have to decide about my future. Deciding to do this, that or the other for the next five, ten or twenty years is no great decision. Turning fully, unconditionally, and without fear to God is. Yet this awareness sets me free.

*Henri J. M. Nouwen*

Life is a grindstone. Whether it grinds you down or polishes you up depends on what you are made of.

*Anon.*

We mustn't be in a hurry to fix and choose our own lot; we must wait to be guided. We are led on, like little children, by a way we know not. It is a vain thought to flee from the work that God appoints us, for the sake of finding a greater blessing to our own souls; as if we could choose for ourselves where we shall find the fullness of the Divine Presence, instead of seeking it where alone it is to be found, in loving obedience.

*George Eliot*

Watch your thoughts, they become words.
Watch your words, they become actions.
Watch your actions, they become habits.
Watch your habits, they become characters.
Watch your character, it becomes your destiny.

*Anon.*

Who may worship in your sanctuary, LORD?
Who may enter your presence on your holy Hill?
Those who lead blameless lives
    and do what is right,
      speaking the truth from sincere hearts.
Those who refuse to slander others
    or harm their neighbours
    or speak evil of their friends.
Those who despise persistent sinners,
    and honour the faithful followers of the LORD
    and keep their promises even when it hurts.
Those who do not charge interest on the money
  they lend,
    and who refuse to accept bribes to testify
      against the innocent.
Such people will stand firm forever.

*Psalm 15 (NLT)*

*I*n the last twenty-five years alone, new inventions
and improvements have utterly transformed the
way we live. Personal computers and fax
machines, cordless phones and wireless speakers, e-
mail and other hi-tech labour-saving conveniences
have revolutionised our work and home life. Yet
have they brought us the peace and freedom they
seemed to promise?

    Without realising it, we have become dulled, if
not brainwashed, in our eagerness to embrace
technology. We have become slaves to a system that
presses us to spend money on new gadgets, and we
have accepted without question the argument that,

by working harder, we will have more time to do the important things. It is a perverse logic. When upgrades on everything from software packages to cars keep us on the constant run, when we are always struggling to keep up with the Joneses (even against our better judgement), we ought to ask ourselves what we have saved, and whether our lives are any more peaceful.

If anything, the increasing complexity of life today has robbed us of peace and resulted in a quiet but widespread epidemic of nervousness, insecurity, and confusion. Fifty years ago German educator Friedrich Wilhelm Foerster wrote:

> More than ever before, our technical civilisation has cushioned life on all sides, yet more than ever, people helplessly succumb to blows of life. This is very simply because a mere material, technical culture cannot give help in the face of tragedy. The man of today, externalised as he is, has no ideas, no strength, to enable him to master his own restlessness and division. He does not know what to make of suffering – how to make something constructive of it – and perceives it only as something that oppresses and exasperates him and interferes with his life. He has no peace. And the same experiences that might help a person with an active inner life gain mastery over life may be enough to send him into a mental institution.

*Taken from* Seeking Peace *by Johann C. Arnold*

Work is not always required of a man. There is
such a thing as a sacred idleness, the
cultivation of which is now fearfully neglected.

*George MacDonald*

Let us be content, in work,
To do the thing we can, and not presume
To fret because it's little.

*Elizabeth Barrett Browning*

I wait quietly before God,
for my salvation comes from Him.
He alone is my rock and my salvation,
My fortress where I will never be shaken.

So many enemies against one man –
all of them trying to kill me.
To them I'm just a broken down wall
or a tottering fence.
They plan to topple me from my high position.
They delight in telling lies about me.
They are friendly to my face,
But they curse me in their hearts.

I wait quietly before God,
For my hope is in him.
He alone is my rock and my salvation,
My fortress where I will not be shaken.
My salvation and my honour come from
    God alone.
He is my refuge, a rock where no enemy can
    reach me.

O my people, trust in him at all times.
Pour out your heart to him,
For God is our refuge.

From the greatest to the lowliest –
All are nothing in his sight.
If you weigh them on the scales,
They are lighter than a puff of air.

Don't try to get rich by extortion or robbery,
And if your wealth increases
don't make it the centre of your life.

God has spoken plainly,
    and I have heard it many times:
Power, O God, belongs to you;
    unfailing love, O Lord, is yours.
Surely you judge all the people
    according to what they have done.

*Psalm 62 (NLT)*

God has given us two hands – one to receive and the other to give to others. We are not cisterns made for hoarding; we are channels made for sharing. If we fail to fulfil this divine duty and privilege we have missed the meaning of Christianity.

*Billy Graham*

## SERVICE

This is the true joy of life: being used up for a purpose recognised by yourself as a mighty one; being a force of nature instead of a feverish, selfish little clod of ailments and grievances, complaining that the world will not devote itself to making you happy.

I am of the opinion that my life belongs to others, and as long as I live, it is my privilege to do for them whatever I can. I want to be thoroughly used up when I die, for the harder I work, the more I live …

Life is no brief candle to me. It is a sort of splendid torch which I have got hold of for a moment, and I want to make it burn as brightly as possible before handing it on to future generations.

*George Bernard Shaw*

I've been a great deal happier since I have given up thinking about what is easy and pleasant, and being discontented because I couldn't have my own will. Our life is determined for us; and it makes the mind very free when we've given up wishing, and only think of bearing what is laid upon us, and doing what is given to us to do.

*George Eliot*


To enjoy your work and accept your lot in life – that is indeed a gift from God. People who do this rarely look with sorrow on the past, for God has given them reasons for joy.

*Ecclesiastes 5:19–20 (NLT)*


Contentment makes much of little; greed makes little of much. Contentment is the poor man's riches and desire the rich man's poverty.

*John Quincy Adams*


We should have great peace if we did not busy ourselves with what others say and do.

*Thomas à Kempis*

*I have learnt, through life's experiences, not to speculate. We tend to pre-suppose how things might be, but the reality is often very different. We bargain without the Grace of God, forgetting that 'His grace is sufficient'.*

The crosses of the present moment always bring their own special grace and consequent comfort with them; we see the hand of God in them when it is laid upon us. But the crosses of anxious foreboding are seen out of the dispensation of God; we see them without grace to bear them; we see them indeed through a faithless spirit, which banishes grace. So, everything in them is bitter and unendurable; all seems dark and helpless. Let us throw self aside; no more self-interest, and then God's will, unfolding every moment in everything, will console us also every moment for all that He shall do around us, or within us, for our discipline.

*Fénelon*

What time I am afraid, I will trust in thee.

*Psalm 56:3 (AV)*

Late on me, weeping, did this whisper fall:
'Dear child, there is no need to weep at all!
Why go about to grieve and to despair?
Why weep now through thy Future's eyes,
    and bear
In vain today tomorrow's load of care?'

*H. S. Sutton*


## IT COULDN'T BE DONE

Somebody said that it couldn't be done,
But he with a chuckle replied
That 'maybe it couldn't,' but he would be one
Who wouldn't say so till he'd tried.
So he buckled right in with the trace of a grin
On his face. If he worried he hid it.
He started to sing as he tackled the thing
That couldn't be done, and he did it.
… There are thousands to tell you it cannot be
    done,
There are thousands to prophesy failure;
There are thousands to point out to you, one
    by one,
The dangers that wait to assail you.
But just buckle in with a bit of a grin,
Just take off your coat and go to it;
Just start to sing as you tackle the thing
That 'cannot be done,' and you'll do it.

*Anon.*

One should take good care not to grow too wise for so great a pleasure of life as laughter.

*John Addison*

This may come as a revelation to you, but you're supposed to get tired! Fatigue is a God-given boundary; otherwise you'd push yourself over the edge.

What is it that gives you acid in your stomach, knots in your neck and makes you less-than-a-joy to be around? Here are three leading contenders: (1) Imagination. It's like virtual reality – it'll make you fear the worst or hold arguments with people who aren't even around to hear them. Ever do that? (2) Memory. It'll keep you stuck in the past. Only by forgiving can you close the door and move on. (3) Impatience. Do slow people make you angry? How about slow traffic? Or slow service in a restaurant? Or a slow supermarket checkout whose till runs out of paper and calls for a price check that nobody can find?

Jesus said, 'Stop allowing yourselves to be agitated' (John 14:27, *Amplified Bible*). You're doing it to yourself! Your unwillingness to accept life as it is will only keep your blood pressure high and your contentment levels low.

You're approaching things from the

world's perspective instead of God's. Listen:
'In the world your shall have ... frustration;
but be of good cheer ... I have deprived it of
power to harm ... you' (John 16:33,
*Amplified Bible*).

*Bob Gass, from* The Word for Today

Everywhere and at all times it is in thy power
piously to acquiesce in thy present condition,
and to behave justly to those who are about
thee.

*Marcus Antoninus*

# CHAPTER FOUR

# *In deeper reverence, praise*

\* \* \*

For the angel of the LORD guards all who
fear him.

*Psalm 34:7 (NLT)*

We have come very safely – hitherto;
And sometimes seas were calm, and skies
    were blue;
Sometimes the wild waves rose – the tempest
    roared;
But never barque went down with Christ
    on board.

And so it shall be to the very end –
Through ebb or flow, the one unchanging
    Friend,
Ruling the waves which sink at His command,
Holding them in the hollow of His hand.

There comes an hour, when, every tempest
    o'er
The harbour lights are reached, the golden
    shores:
Never, oh nevermore to fret or fear –
Christ, give us faith to praise Thee
    even here!

*Mary Gorges*

You will keep in perfect peace all who trust in you,
    whose thoughts are fixed on you!
Trust in the LORD always,
    For the LORD GOD is the eternal Rock.

*Isaiah 26:3–4 (NLT)*

I am so glad! It is such rest to know
That Thou hast ordered and appointed all
And wilt yet order and appoint my lot.
For though so much I cannot understand,
And would not choose, has been, and yet may be,
Thou choosest, Thou performest, thou, my Lord,
This is enough for me.

*Frances R. Havergal*

## THE MORNING HOUR

Alone with God, in quiet peace,
From earthly cares I find release;
New strength I borrow from each day
As there with God, I stop to pray.

Alone with God, my sins confess'd
He speaks in mercy, I am blest.
I know the kiss of pardon free,
I talk to God, He talks to me.

Alone with God, my vision clears
I see my guilt, the wasted years
I plead for grace to walk His way
And live for Him, from day to day.

Alone with God, no sin between
His lovely face so plainly seen;
My guilt all gone, my heart at rest
With Christ, my Lord, my soul is blest.

Lord, keep my life alone for Thee;
From sin and self, Lord, set me free.
And when no more this earth I trod
They'll say, 'He walked alone with God.'

*Anon.*

Let us all become a true and fruitful branch
    on the vine Jesus,
By accepting Him in our lives as it pleases
    Him to come:
as the Truth - to be told;
as the Life – to be lived;
as the Light – to be lighted;
as the Love – to be loved;
as the Way – to be walked;
as the Joy – to be given;
as the Peace – to be spread;
as the Sacrifice – to be offered,
in our families and within our neighbourhood.

*Mother Teresa*

Glory to Thee, my God, this night
For all the blessings of the light;
Keep me, O keep me, King of kings,
Beneath Thine own almighty wings.

Forgive me, Lord, for Thy dear Son,
The ill that I this day have done,
That with the world, myself, and Thee,
I, ere I sleep, at peace may be.

Teach me to live, that I may dread
The grave as little as my bed;
Teach me to die, that so I may
Rise glorious at the awful day.

O may my soul on Thee repose,
And may sweet sleep mine eyelids close,
Sleep that shall me more vigorous make
To serve my God when I awake.

When in the night I sleepless lie,
My soul with heavenly thoughts supply;
Let no ill dreams disturb my rest,
No powers of darkness me molest.

Praise God, from Whom all blessings flow,
Praise Him all creatures here below,
Praise Him above, ye heav'nly host,
Praise Father, Son and Holy Ghost.

*Thomas Ken*

# CHAPTER FIVE

# *In simple trust, like theirs who heard ...*

\* \* \*

In trust, such as those who heard Jesus calling to them and who simply got up and followed Him ...(paraphrase mine)

Whenever I read about the way Jesus chose his disciples I marvel at the charisma of a man who could cause rugged fishermen and tax collectors to drop everything – all they had ever known to provide them with a living – and decide to follow him! That's trust!

These men, who became Jesus' disciples, were not attracted to him because he had a set of rules or religious fervour, but because his very life spoke to them of reality, love and truth.

It is also a mystery, because however many facts we have about Jesus, every person has to take that one step of blind faith without knowing that it will be the best decision they ever make.

Wise men still follow him.

*Anon.*

O little town of Bethlehem,
How still we see thee lie!
Above thy deep and dreamless sleep
The silent stars go by:
Yet in thy dark streets shineth
The everlasting Light;
The hopes and fears of all the years.
Are met in thee tonight.

For Christ is born of Mary;
And gathered all above,
While mortals sleep, the angels keep,
Their watch of wondering love.
O morning stars, together
Proclaim the holy birth,
And praises sing to God the King,
And peace to men on earth.

How silently, how silently,
The wondrous gift is given!
So, God imparts to human hearts
The blessings of His heaven.
No ear may hear His coming;
But in this world of sin.
Where meek souls will receive Him, still,
The dear Christ enters in.

O holy Child of Bethlehem,
Descend to us, we pray;
Cast out our sin, and enter in:
Be born in us today.
We hear the Christmas angels,
The great glad tidings tell:
O come to us, abide with us,
Our Lord Emmanuel.

*Bishop Phillips Brooks*

*This is one of my favourite Christmas hymns; not because of the variety of tunes it is sung to, but because of the words. I believe that if every person who sang these words at Christmas time really meant them, millions of lives would be transformed and the world would be very different as a result.*

Let us, like them, without a word,
Rise up and follow thee.

For a child is born to us, a son is given to us
And the government will rest on his shoulders.
These will be his royal titles: Wonderful
Counsellor, Mighty God, Everlasting Father,
Prince of Peace. His ever expanding, peaceful
government will never end.

*The birth of Jesus, prophesied by Isaiah
(9:6–7, NLT)*

When Jesus came into the world, peace was
sung; and when he went out of the world,
peace was bequeathed.

*Francis Bacon*

Suddenly, the angel was joined by a vast host
of others – the armies of heaven – praising
God:

'Glory to God in the highest heaven,
    and peace on earth to all whom God
favours.'

*Luke 2:14 (NLT)*

## CHRISTMAS BELLS

I heard the bells on Christmas day
Their old familiar carols play,
And wild and sweet
The words repeat,
Of 'Peace on earth, good will to men!'

And thought how, as the day had come,
The belfries of all Christendom
Had rolled along
The unbroken song,
Of 'Peace on earth, good will to men!'

Till ringing, singing on its way,
The world revolved from night to day –
A voice, a chime,
A chant sublime,
Of 'Peace on earth, good will to men!'

And in despair I bowed my head;
'There is no peace on earth,' I said,
'For hate is strong
And mocks the song
Of "Peace on earth, good will to men!"'

Then pealed the bells more loud and deep:
'God is not dead; nor doth he sleep!
The wrong shall fail,
The right prevail,
With peace on earth, good will to men!'

*Henry Wadsworth Longfellow*


What kind of greatness can this be,
That chose to be made small?
Exchanging untold majesty
For a world so pitiful.
That God should come as one of us
I'll never understand
The more I hear the story
The more amazed I am.

The One in whom we live and move,
In swaddling clothes lies bound.
The voice that cried 'Let there be light,'
Asleep without a sound.
The One who strode among the stars,
And called each one by name
Lies helpless in a mother's arms
And must learn to walk again.

What greater love could He have shown
To shamed humanity
Yet human pride hates to believe
In such deep humility.
But nations now may see His grace
And know that He is near,
When His meek heart, his words, his works
Are incarnate in us here.

*Graham Kendrick*

*I remember singing this old chorus with my husband Roy at a Christian event. It was made famous by Cliff Barrows who sang at all the Billy Graham crusades – words are simple, sentiments divine!*

> I have decided to follow Jesus.
> I have decided to follow Jesus.
> I have decided to follow Jesus.
> No turning back, no turning back.

> The world behind me, the cross before me ...
> No turning back, no turning back.

> Tho' none go with me, still I will follow ...
> No turning back, no turning back.

> Will you decide now, to follow Jesus? ...
> No turning back, no turning back.

> *Anon.*

Neither go back in fear and misgiving to the past, nor in anxiety and forecasting to the future; but lie quiet under His hand, having no will but His.

*Henry Manning*

Begin at once; before you venture away from this quiet moment, ask your King to take you wholly into His service, and place all the hours of this day quite simply at his disposal, and ask Him to make and keep you *ready* to do just exactly what He appoints. Never mind about tomorrow; one day at a time is enough. Try it today, and see if it is not a day of strange, almost curious peace, so sweet that you will be only too thankful, when tomorrow comes, to ask Him to take it also – till it will become a blessed habit to hold yourself simply and 'wholly at Thy commandment for any manner of service'. The 'whatsoever' is not necessarily active work. It may be waiting (whether half an hour or half a lifetime), learning, suffering, sitting still. But shall we be less ready for these, if any of them are His appointments for today? Let us ask Him to prepare us for all that He is preparing for us.

*Frances R. Havergal*

# CHAPTER SIX

# *O sabbath rest by Galilee*

\* \* \*

*It was in the hills by the Sea of Galilee that Jesus sat to speak to the crowds of people who had gathered to learn from this amazing teacher. I remember someone commenting that if we obeyed the teaching from the Sermon on the Mount alone, we'd be perfect!*

*He begins with the Be(autiful) attitudes:*

God blesses those who realize their need
 for him,
 for the Kingdom of Heaven is given to them.
God blesses those who mourn,
 for they will be comforted.
God blesses those who are gentle and lowly,
 for the whole earth will belong to them.
God blesses those who are hungry and thirsty
 for justice,
 for they will receive it in full.
God blesses those who are merciful,
 for they will be shown mercy.
God blesses those whose hearts are pure,
 for they will see God.
God blesses those who work for peace,
 for they will be called the children of God.

God blesses those who are persecuted because
    they live for God,
  for the Kingdom of Heaven is theirs.

God blesses you when you are mocked and
persecuted and lied about because you are my
followers. Be happy about it! Be very glad! For
a great reward awaits you in heaven. And
remember the ancient prophets were
persecuted too!

*Matthew 5:3–12 (NLT)*

Blessed are the peacemakers: for they shall
be called the children of God.

*Matthew 5:9 (AV)*

Who brings about peace is called the
companion of God in the work of creation.

*Jewish saying*

Have you ever thought seriously of the meaning of that blessing given to the peacemakers? People are always expecting to get peace in heaven; but you know whatever peace they get will be ready-made. Whatever making of peace they can be blest for, must be on the earth here: not the taking of arms against, but the building of nests amidst, it's sea of troubles (like the halcyons). Difficult enough, you think? Perhaps so, but I do not see that any of us try. We complain of the want of many things – we want votes, we want liberty, we want amusement, we want money. Which of us feels or knows that he wants peace?

*John Ruskin*

Peacemaking is a noble vocation. But you can no more make peace in your own strength than a mason can build a wall without a trowel, a carpenter build a house without a hammer, or an artist paint a picture without a brush. You must have the proper equipment. To be a peacemaker, you must know the Peace Giver. To make peace on earth, you must know the peace of heaven. You must know Him who 'is our peace'.

*Billy Graham*

O God, who art Peace everlasting, whose chosen reward is the gift of peace, and hast taught us that the peacemakers are Thy children, pour Thy sweet peace into our souls, that everything discordant may utterly vanish, and all that makes for peace be sweet to us forever.

*Gelasian*

Our first step as peacemaker is toward ourselves. Most of us find it difficult to initiate peace with others because we are not at peace with the person who lives in our own skin. We need to meet that unique person inside. Often we are harder on that person than anyone else.

We find it difficult to forgive ourselves, even after we've heard and accepted the forgiveness of the cross. But it is blasphemy to contradict the Lord, and He has loved us unreservedly. We need to ask him to help us to love ourselves as much as He does. That also will free us of self-condemnation, negation, and lambasting.

A test of our acceptance of us as Christ-loved and forgiven persons will be abiding peace. A profound centre of calm is the result of creative delight and enjoyment of ourselves. Happy are the peacemakers – with themselves.

The natural overflow of that inner peace will be a transformed attitude toward the people around us. Then we can become initiating peacemakers with others. That ministry has three parts: making peace between us and others; between people we know who are separated from one another because of misunderstanding, hurt and hatred; and between groups in our society.

*J. Lloyd Ogilvie, from* Turning Your Struggles into Stepping Stones

First keep yourself in peace, and then you will be able to pacify others.

*Thomas à Kempis*

How shall we rest in God? By giving ourselves wholly to Him. If you give yourself by halves, you cannot find full rest; there will ever be a lurking disquiet in that half which is withheld. Martyrs, confessors, and saints have tasted this rest, and 'counted them-selves happy in that they endured'. A countless host of God's faithful servants have drunk deeply of it under the daily burdens of a weary life – dull, commonplace, painful, or desolate. All that God has been to them He is ready to be to you. The heart once fairly given to God, with a clear conscience, a fitting rule of life, and a steadfast purpose of obedience, you will find a wonderful sense of rest coming over you.

*Jean Nicolas Grou*

So there is a Sabbath rest still waiting for the people of God. For all who enter into God's rest will find rest from their labours, just as God rested after creating the world.

*Hebrews 4:9–10 (NLT)*

Calm soul of all things! Make it mine
To feel, amid the city's jar,
That there abides a peace of thine,
Man did not make, and cannot mar.

*Matthew Arnold*

Peace is not just passivity. It is not merely stagnation. It is not sterility. It is not a negative attitude of non-involvement.

The production of peace calls for powerful and a most pronounced action on the part of the peacemaker. The path of peace which God's Word instructs us to pursue is not strewn softly with rose petals. Rather it is a tough trail tramped out with humble heart and lowly spirit despite its rough rocks of adversity.

*W. Phillip Keller, from* A Gardener Looks at the Fruits of the Spirit

May God our Father and the Lord Jesus Christ give you His grace and peace.

*1 Corinthians 1:3 (NLT)*

# CHAPTER SEVEN

# O calm of hills above

\* \* \*

*I have asked friends what the word 'peace' means to them and popular answers have been:*

- *Outdoors, with nature;*
- *A walk in the woods;*
- *The mountains of Switzerland;*
- *In my garden; by the sea.*

*In other words, peaceful surroundings.*

*My husband loved his garden. He found great solace there. The cares and stresses of his life would recede and time would disappear! Only a parched throat or rumbling tummy would remind him that time had passed. Something that is in contrast to everyday life and its pressures can bring peace.*

*I think there must be some truth in the well-worn poem:*

> The kiss of the sun for pardon,
> The song of the birds for mirth,
> One is nearer to God in a garden
> Than anywhere else on earth.
>
> *Dorothy Frances Gurney*

## MY GARDEN

A garden is a lovesome thing, God wot!
Rose plot,
Fringed pool,
Fern'd grot –
The veriest school
Of peace; and yet the fool
Contends that God is not –
Not God! In gardens! When the eve is cool?
Nay, but I have a sign;
'Tis very sure God walks in mine.

*Thomas Edward Brown*


A man whispered, 'God, speak to me,' and a meadowlark sang. But the man did not hear.

The man yelled, 'God, speak to me!' And the thunder rolled across the sky. But the man did not listen.

The man looked around and said, 'God, let me see You.' And a star shone brightly. But the man did not notice.

And the man shouted, 'God, show me a miracle!' And a life was born. But the man did not know.

So the man cried out in despair, 'Touch me, God, and let me know You are here!' Whereupon God reached down and touched the man. But the man brushed the butterfly away and walked on.

*Barbara Johnson*

## LINES WRITTEN IN EARLY SPRING

I heard a thousand blended notes,
While in a grove I sate reclined,
In that sweet mood when pleasant thoughts
Bring sad thoughts to the mind.

To her fair works did nature link
The human soul that through me ran;
And much it grieved my heart to think
What man has made of man.

Through primrose-tufts, in that sweet bower,
The periwinkle trailed its wreathes;
And 'tis my faith that every flower
Enjoys the air it breathes.

The birds around me hopped and played:
Their thoughts I cannot measure,
But the least motion which they made,
It seemed a thrill of pleasure.

The budding twigs spread out their fan.
To catch the breezy air;
And I must think, do all I can,
That there was pleasure there.

If I these thoughts may not prevent,
If such be of my creed the plan,
Have I not reason to lament
What man has made of man?

*William Wordsworth*

Go out into the woods and valleys, when your heart is rather harassed than bruised, and when you suffer from vexation rather than grief. Then the trees all hold out their arms to you to relieve you of the burden of your heavy thoughts. And the streams under the trees glance at you as they run by, and will carry away your trouble along with the fallen leaves.

*Robert Vaughan*


## THE WAY THROUGH THE WOODS

They shut the road through the woods
Seventy years ago.
Weather and rain have undone it again,
And now you would never know
There was once a road through the woods
Before they planted the trees.
It is underneath the coppice and heath
And the thin anemones.
Only the keeper sees
That, where the ring-dove broods,
And the badgers roll at ease,
There was once a road through the woods.

Yet, if you enter the woods
On a summer evening late,
When the night air cools on the trout-
    ringed pools
Where the otter whistles his mate,
(They fear not men in the woods,
Because they see so few)
You will hear the beat of a horse's feet,
And the swish of a skirt in the dew,
Steadily cantering through
The misty solitudes,
As they perfectly knew
The old lost road through the woods ...
But there is no road through the woods.

*Rudyard Kipling*


The year's at the spring,
And day's at the morn;
Morning's at seven;
The hillside's dew-pearled;
The lark's on the wing;
The snail's on the thorn:
God's in His heaven –
All's right with the world!

*Robert Browning*

The Lord walks in the cool of the evening,
with those who seek sanctuary there.

*Found on the wall of an old country garden*

## SERENITY

Above green-smocked hills,
birdlife flips and frolics
in impromptu winged ballet,
shapely bosomed land
veiled in drapes, shaded
in yellow, bronze, purple hues,
skirts, styled in chequered greens,
sweep down in elegance
through valleys they overlook,
a silver sash gleams its way
across shoulders and downwards,
like a million sparkling sequins –
devoured by a sunlit river,
nonchalant sheep graze,
monotonous calls float on air
in unknown harmony of peace.

Serenity is framed here,
captured by the eyes,
analysed by the mind,
embraced by the heart,
embalmed by the soul.

*Harry Boyle*

When the voices of children are
heard on the green
And laughter is heard on the hill,
My heart is at rest within my breast
And everything else is still.

*William Blake*


Peace reigns where the Lord reigns.

*Julian of Norwich*


## MORNING GLORY

I arose, and for a space
The scene of woods and waters seemed to keep,
Though it was now broad day, a gentle trace
Of light diviner than the common sun
Sheds on the common earth, and all the place

Was filled with magic sounds woven into one
Oblivious melody, confusing sense
Amid the gliding waves and shadows dun;

And, as I looked, the bright omnipresence
Of morning through the orient cavern flowed,
And the sun's image radiantly intense

Burned on the waters of the well that glowed
Like gold, and threaded all the forest's maze
With winding paths of emerald fire; there stood

Amid the sun, as he amid the blaze
Of his own glory, on the vibrating
Floor of the fountain, paved with flashing rays,

A Shape all light, which with one hand did fling
Dew on the earth, as if she were the dawn,
And the invisible rain did ever sing

A silver music on the mossy lawn ...

*Percy Bysshe Shelley*


Every year after the strain of winter our
whole being begins to ache for all that the
summer means. Quiet Sunday afternoons,
for instance, with a book on a secluded lawn,
the shadow of beeches on the grass, and the
clouds floating slowly across the blue above
our heads, the silence defined rather than
broken by the occasional hum of a bee
passing from flower to flower. 'Like a
walled-in garden to a troubled mind.'

What a description of the peace of God! I
know some gardens that seem to have about
them a secret peace in which the whole
personality seems bathed and restored.

*Leslie D. Weatherhead*

Grant us Thy peace, down from Thy presence falling
As on the thirsty earth cool night-dews sweet;
Grant us Thy peace, to Thy pure paths recalling,
From devious ways, our worn and wandering feet.

*E. Scudder*

A thing of beauty is a joy for ever:
Its loveliness increases; it will never
Pass into nothingness; but still will keep
A bower quiet for us and a sleep
Full of sweet dreams, and health, and
    quiet breathing.

*John Keats*

PEACE

Sitting alone – I daydream,
Swathed in veils of fantasy
I see, I hear – or it would seem,
A world, kind, sincere and free,
Sounds of normal life fade –
No grind of man's machines,
My view is of beauty laid,
Lilting songbirds, whispering streams,
My soul is warmly caressed
By a blue splashed sunlit sky,
Untethered from bonds of stress,

Immersed in happiness am I,
Amidst the fragrance of flowers,
Sweet melodies kiss the breeze,
My heart basks in gentle showers
As hands of friendship reach
Embracing cordiality
Within my fantasy – my peace.

*Harry Boyle*


Great peace is found in little busyness.

*Geoffrey Chaucer*


Nor fear, nor grief, nor vain perplexity,
So will I build my altar in the fields,
And the blue sky my fretted dome shall be,
And the sweet fragrance that the wild flower yields
Shall be the incense I will yield to Thee,
The only God! And thou shalt not despise
Even me, the priest of this poor sacrifice.

*Samuel Taylor Coleridge*

*I love the way Walter de la Mare draws you into
the atmosphere of his poems by his wonderfully
descriptive ability.*

### THE LINNET

Upon this leafy bush
With thorns and roses in it,
Flutters a thing of light,
A twittering linnet,
And all the throbbing world
Of dew and sun and air
By this small parcel of life
Is made more fair;
As if each bramble-spray
And mounded gold-wreathed furze,
Were only hers;
As if this beauty and grace
Did to one bird belong,
And, at a flutter of wing,
Might vanish in song.

*Walter de la Mare*

## SILVER

Slowly, silently, now the moon
Walks the night in her silver shoon;
This way and that she peers, and sees
Silver fruit upon silver trees;
One by one the casements catch
Her beams beneath the silvery thatch.
Couched in his kennel, like a log,
With paws of silver sleeps the dog;
From their shadowy cote the white breasts peep
Of doves in a silver-feathered sleep.
A harvest mouse goes scampering by,
With silver claws and silver eye;
And moveless fish in the waters gleam,
By silver reeds in a silver stream.

*Walter de la Mare*

## NOD

Softly along the road of evening,
In a twilight dim with rose,
Wrinkled with age, and drenched with dew,
Old Nod, the shepherd, goes.

His drowsy flock streams on before him,
Their fleeces charged with gold,
To where the sun's last beam leans low
On Nod the shepherd's fold.

The hedge is quick and green with briar,
From their sand the conies creep;
And all the birds that fly in heaven
Flock singing home to sleep.

His lambs outnumber a noon's roses,
Yet, when night's shadow fall,
His blind old sheep dog, Slumber-soon,
Misses not one of all.

His are the quiet steeps of dreamland,
The waters of no-more-pain,
His ram's bell rings 'neath an arch of stars,
'Rest, rest, and rest again.'

*Walter de la Mare*

The best things are nearest:
Breath in your nostrils, light in your eyes,
Flowers at your feet, duties at your hand
The path of God just before you.

*Robert Louis Stevenson*

# CHAPTER EIGHT

# *Where Jesus knelt to share with thee the silence of eternity*

\*\*\*

*If we follow Jesus' example, we will realise the benefit of drawing aside from the activities and stress of our lives to spend time with God in peace and quiet; not just praying for things we want, but to hear from him what he wants of our lives.*

> To be in Your presence,
> To sit at Your feet
> Where Your love surrounds me,
> And makes me complete.
> This is my desire, O Lord
> This is my desire.
>
> To rest in Your presence,
> Not turning away,
> To cherish each moment,
> Here I would stay.
> This is my desire, O Lord
> This is my desire.

*Noel Richards*

Interpose no barrier to His mighty life-giving power, working in you all the good pleasure of His will. Yield yourself up utterly to His sweet control. Put your growing into His hands as completely as you have put all other affairs. Suffer Him to manage it, as He will. Do not concern yourself about it, not even think of it. Trust Him absolutely and always. Accept each moment's dispensation as it comes to you from His dear hands, as being the needed sunshine or dew for that moment's growth. Say a continual 'yes' to your Father's will.

*Anon.*


Run,
man of the world!
Run to the volume knobs
Of raucous radio,
Silver screen,
And constant chatter.
You dare not stop!
Somehow you've found that silence
Is for hearing
Echoes of emptiness.

Run,
Man of God!
Run to the quiet control
Of bended knees,
Open Bible
And constant communion.
You dare not stop!
Somehow you've found that silence
Is for hearing
God's still voice.

*Susan Lenzkes*

My cell was deep underground. A light bulb
shone from the ceiling on bare walls, an iron
bedstead with three planks and a straw
pallet. Air entered through a pipe high in the
wall. The silence here was practically
complete – deliberately so. Our guards wore
felt-soled shoes and you could hear their
hands on the door before key found lock.
Now and again there was the far-off sound
of a prisoner hammering steadily on his door
or screaming. The cell allowed only three
paces in each direction, so I lay down and
stared at the bulb. It burned all night. Since
I could not sleep, I prayed. The outside
world had ceased to exist. All the noises I
was used to, the wind and rain in the yard,
steel boot studs on stone floors, the buzz of
a fly, a human voice, were gone. My heart

97

seemed to shrink, as if it too would stop in this lifeless silence.

I was kept in solitary confinement in this cell for the next two years. I had nothing to read and no writing materials; I had only my thoughts for company, and I was not a meditative man, but a soul that had rarely known quiet. I had God. But had I really lived to serve God – or was it simply my profession? Now the test had come. I was alone. There was no salary to earn, no golden opinions to consider. God offered me only suffering – would I continue to love Him? ...

I wondered how you could praise God by a life of silence. At first I prayed gently to be released. I asked, 'You have said in Scripture that it is not good that a man should be alone; why do You keep me alone?' But as days passed into weeks my only visitor was still the guard, who brought wedges of black bread and watery soup and never spoke a word ...

Slowly I learned that on the tree of silence hangs the fruit of peace. I began to realise my real personality, and made sure that it belonged to Christ. I found that even here my thoughts and feelings turned to God and that I could pass night after night in prayer, spiritual exercise and praise. I knew now that I was not play-acting, believing that I believed.

*Richard Wurmbrand, from*
From God's Underworld

The soul would have no rainbows, if the eye
had no tears.

*Anon.*

How still, how happy! Those are words
That once would scarce agree together;
I loved the plashing of the surge,
The changing heaven, the breezy weather,

More than smooth seas and cloudless skies
And solemn, soothing, softened airs
That in the forest woke no sighs
And from the green spray shook no tears.

How still, how happy! Now I feel
Where silence dwells is sweeter far
Than laughing mirth's most joyous swell
However pure its raptures are.

Come, sit down on this sunny stone:
'Tis wintry light o'er flowerless moors –
But sit – for we are all alone
And clear expand heaven's breathless shores.

*Emily Brontë*

What is the quiet mind? A quiet mind is one which nothing weighs on, nothing worries, which, free from ties and all self-seeking, is wholly merged into the will of God and dead to its own.

*Meister Eckhart*

Thine own self-will and anxiety, thy hurry and labour, disturb thy peace and prevent Me from working in thee. Look at the little flowers, in the serene summer days; they quietly open their petals, and the sun shines into them with his gentle influences. So will I do for thee, if thou wilt yield thyself to Me.

*G. Tersteegen*

Go placidly amid the noise and the haste, and remember what peace there may be in silence.

*Max Ehrmann*

## SOLITUDE

Happy the man, whose wish and care
A few paternal acres bound,
Content to breathe his native air
In his own ground.

Whose herds with milk, whose fields with bread,
Whose flocks supply him with attire;
Whose trees in summer yield him shade,
In winter fire.

Blest, who can unconcerned'ly find
Hours, days, and years slide soft away
In health of body, peace of mind,
Quiet by day

Sound sleep by night; study and ease
Together mix'd, sweet recreation,
And innocence, which most does please
with meditation.

Thus let me live, unseen, unknown;
Thus unlamented let me die;
Steal from the world, and not a stone
Tell where I lie.

*Alexander Pope*

'Do not let your hearts be troubled. Trust in God; trust also in me. In my Father's house are many rooms; if it were not so, I would have told you. I am going there to prepare a place for you. And if I go and prepare a place for you, I will come back and take you to be with me that you also may be where I am. You know the way to the place where I am going.'

Thomas said to him, 'Lord, we don't know where you are going, so how can we know the way?'

Jesus answered, 'I am the way and the truth and the life. No-one comes to the Father except through me.'

*John 14:1–6 (NIV)*

*These words of Jesus give us, as Christians, the hope and assurance that eternity is secured, through him. The following prayer, which I remember saying at evensong in my schooldays, also assures us of peace in eternity.*

O Lord, support us all the day long of this troublous life, until the shades lengthen and the evening comes, the busy world is hushed, the fever of life is over, and our work done.

Then, Lord, in Thy mercy, grant us safe lodging, a holy rest, and peace at the last, through Jesus Christ, our Lord, Amen.

*John Henry Newman*

Go forth to meet the solemnities and to conquer the trials of existence, believing in a Shepherd of your souls. Then faith in Him will support you in duty, and duty firmly done will strengthen faith; till at last, when all is over here, and the noise and strife of the earthly battle fades upon your dying ear, and you hear, instead thereof, the deep and musical sound of the ocean of eternity. And see the lights of heaven shining on its waters still and fair in their radiant rest, your faith will raise the song of conquest, and in its retrospect of the life which has ended, and its forward glance upon the life to come, take up the poetic inspiration of the Hebrew King, 'Surely goodness and mercy have followed me all the days of my life and I will dwell in the house of the Lord forever.'

*Stopford A. Brooke*

Guide us through life; and when at last
We enter into rest,
Thy tender arms about us cast,
And fold us to Thy breast.

*H. F. Lyte*

'Where, O death, is your victory? Where, O death, is your sting?'

The sting of death is sin, and the power of sin is the law. But thanks be to God! He gives us the victory through our Lord Jesus Christ.

*1 Corinthians 15:55–57 (NIV)*

## JOHN ADAMS MOVES OUT

In a diary entry in 1814 the former present of the United States John Quincy Adams wrote, 'My hopes of a future life are all founded upon the gospel of Jesus Christ.' In 1846, on the occasion of his seventy-ninth birthday, Adams wrote, 'I enter my eightieth year, with thanksgiving to God for all the blessings and mercies which His providence has bestowed upon me throughout a life extended now to the longest term allotted to the life of man.'

After that time a friend met Adams on the street, shook his trembling hand, and said, 'Good morning, and how is John Quincy Adams today?'

Adams replied, 'He himself is quite well, sir, quite well. But the house in which he lives at the present is becoming dilapidated.

It is tottering upon its foundation. Time and the seasons have almost destroyed it. Its roof is pretty well worn, its walls are much shattered, and it crumbles a bit more with every wind. The old tenement is becoming almost uninhabitable and I think John Quincy Adams will have to move out of it soon; but he himself is well, sir, quite well.' Several weeks later John Quincy Adams suffered a stroke and moved to an imperishable home in heaven.

Christ lives and He has promised everlasting life to all who trust in Him. No matter what happens in this earthly life, we too can give thanks to Him and say that we are well, quite well.

*Taken from* Generation to Generation
*by Kelin E. Gersick et al*

My storm-swept soul is calm at last. These words of peace God speaks to me: 'Thou wilt keep him in perfect peace whose mind is stayed on thee.'

*Flora Sorenson*

Remember! – It is Christianity to do good always – even to those who do evil to us. It is Christianity to love our neighbour as ourself, and to do to all men as we would have them do to us.

It is Christianity to be gentle, merciful, and forgiving, and to keep those qualities quiet in our own heart, and never make a boast of them, or of our prayers or of our love of God, but always to show that we love Him by humbly trying to do right in everything. If we do this, and remember the life and lessons of our Lord Jesus Christ, and try to act up to them, we may confidently hope that God will forgive us our sins and mistakes, and enable us to live and die in Peace.

*Charles Dickens*

Where now with pain thou treadest, trod
The whitest of the saints of God!
To show thee where their feet were set,
The light which led them shineth yet.

*J. G. Whittier*

## THE HILLS ON WHICH I NEED TO GAZE

I climbed the hill
Through yesterday:
And I am young
And strong again;
My children climb
These hills with me,
and all the time
they shout and play;
their laughter fills
the coves among
the rhododendron and the oak
till we have struggled to
the ridge top
where the chestnuts grèw.
Breathless, tired and content
we let the mountain
breeze blow through
our busy minds
and through our hair
refresh our bodies hot and spent
and drink
from some cool mountain spring
the view refreshing everything –
Infinity, with hill between,
Silent, lazy, wild – serene,
Then …
When I return to now
I pray,
'Thank you God
for yesterday.'

*Ruth Bell Graham,*
*from* Sitting by My Laughing Fire

The comfort of a mind at rest
From every care Thou hast not blest;
A heart from all the world set free,
To worship and to wait on Thee.

*A. L. Waring*

# CHAPTER NINE

# *Interpreted by love*

\* \* \*

How deep the Father's love for us
How vast beyond all measure,
That He should give His only Son
To make this wretch a treasure.
How great the pain of searing loss
The Father turns His face away,
As wounds which mar the chosen One
Bring many sons to glory.

Behold the Man upon a cross
My sin upon His shoulders
Ashamed, I hear my mocking voice
Call out among the scoffers.
It was my sin that nailed Him there
Until it was accomplished;
His dying breath has brought me life
I know that it is finished.

I will not boast in anything,
No gifts, no power, no wisdom;
But I will boast in Jesus Christ;
His death and resurrection.
Why should I gain from His reward?
I cannot give an answer.
But this I know with all my heart
His wounds have paid my ransom.

*Stuart Townend*

Such love has no fear because perfect love expels all fear.

*1 John 4:18 (NLT)*

Just as I am, without one plea
But that Thy blood was shed for me,
And that Thou bidst me come to Thee,
O Lamb of God, I come.

Just as I am, though tossed about
With many a conflict, many a doubt,
Fightings within, and fears without,
O Lamb of God, I come.

Just as I am, poor, wretched, blind,
Sight, riches, healing of the mind,
Yea, all I need, in Thee to find,
O Lamb of God, I come.

Just as I am, thou wilt receive,
Wilt welcome, pardon, cleanse, relieve,
Because Thy promise I believe,
O Lamb of God, I come.

Just as I am (Thy love unknown
Has broken every barrier down),
Now to be Thine, yea, Thine alone,
O Lamb of God, I come.

Just as I am, of that free love
The breadth, length, depth, and height to prove,
Here for a season, then above,
O Lamb of God, I come.

*Charlotte Elliott*

# CHAPTER TEN

# Drop thy still dews of quietness

✳ ✳ ✳

*If we prayed this beautiful verse of the hymn every morning, before the busyness of the day began, we might find it speaking deep into our spirits, enabling us to remain calm amid the storms of life.*

Let us then labour for an inward stillness –
An inward stillness and an inward healing;
That perfect silence, where the lips and heart
Are still, and we no longer entertain
Our own imperfect thoughts and vain opinions,
But God alone speaks in us, and we wait
In singleness of heart, that we may know
His will, and in the silence of our spirits
That we may do His will, and do that only.

*Henry Wadsworth Longfellow*

'Oh, that you had listened to my commands! Then you would have had peace flowing like a gentle river and righteousness flowing like waves.'

*Isaiah 48:18 (NLT)*

And do not set your heart on what you will eat or drink; do not worry about it. For the pagan world runs after all such things, and your Father knows that you need them. But seek his kingdom, and these things will be given to you as well.

*Luke 12:29–31 (NIV)*

Jedburgh Abbey is just across the border in Scotland. It's a lovely tranquil place. The ruined walls in warm red stone, their corners smoothed by centuries of wind and rain. A visitor once wrote: '*Everywhere peace, everywhere serenity, and a marvellous freedom from the tumult of the world.*'

The words have a modern ring to them but they were written 850 years ago. The longing for peace and quiet isn't new.

Walking around the ruins I tried to imagine what 'the tumult of the world' really was all that time ago. The loudest noise then would have been a clap of thunder, the loudest human made noise church bells. No motorway traffic, no hi-fi at fifty watts playing through open summer windows.

But I guess it was the demands of everyday life that the writer was thinking of. The demands people made on his time, energy and sympathies. His daily routine and the occasional crisis.

Nothing much changes. They're the same demands on us today. Family concerns, the pressures of work or looking for work, meeting others' expectations. Most of us yearn for something different. We look back to an ideal past when we think life was quiet and peaceful. But it wasn't and we have to live in the now. Today is where we begin, and whether it's good or not, whether we like it or not, that's what we have to work with. We can only come to terms with the tumult of our world by facing it, not by wishing it away.

*Eddie Askew, from* Slower than Butterflies


Sweet are the thoughts that savour of content:
The quiet mind is richer than a crown.

*Robert Greene*

How blessed is he who leads a country life,
Unvex'd with anxious cares and void of strife!
Who, studying peace and shunning civil rage,
Enjoy'd his youth, and now enjoy'd his age:
All who deserve his love, he makes his own;
And, to be loved himself, needs only to be known.

*John Dryden*

Prayer is the peace of our spirit,
The stillness of our thoughts,
The evenness of our recollection,
The seat of our meditation,
The rest of our cares
And the calm of our tempest.

*Jeremy Taylor*

Quiet minds cannot be perplexed or frightened, but go on in fortune or misfortune at
their own private pace, like a clock during a
thunderstorm.

*Robert Louis Stevenson*

# CHAPTER ELEVEN

# Till all our strivings cease

\* \* \*

*D*id you hear the story of the man who climbed
the ladder of success only to find, when he got
to the top, that it had been leaning against the
wrong wall?

So many times we strive for things that will
bring us no lasting satisfaction, and many of our
struggles are self-imposed.

Grant, O Lord my God, that I may never fall
away in success or failure; that I may not be
prideful in prosperity nor dejected in adversity.
Let me rejoice only in what unites us and
sorrow only in what separates us. May I strive
to please no one or fear to displease anyone
except Yourself. May I seek always the things
which are eternal and never those that are only
temporal.

*St Thomas Aquinas*

*V*ery shortly after becoming a Christian, God began to help me sort out my priorities. He also showed me, through Psalm 32, that he had a plan and a purpose for my life.

> The LORD says, 'I will guide you along the best pathway for your life. I will advise you and watch over you.'
>
> *Psalm 32:8 (NLT)*

*I*was a mother of four young children, and he showed me that my family were my priority. So long as I was doing the job God wanted me to do, that *would be my place of peace – no matter how humdrum, repetitive or unnoticed that job was. I have proved the truth of 'my place of peace' for many years now.*

> My future is in your hands.
>
> *Psalm 31:15 (NLT)*

If I did not simply live from one moment to the next, it would be impossible for me to keep my patience. I can see only the present, I forget the past and I take good care not to think about the future. We get discouraged and feel despair because we brood about the past and the future. It is such folly to pass one's time fretting, instead of quietly resting on the heart of Jesus.

*St Thérèse of Lisieux*

Don't worry about tomorrow, for tomorrow will bring its own worries. Today's trouble is enough for today.

*Matthew 6:34 (NLT)*

Today is the tomorrow you worried about yesterday and all is well!

*Anon.*

> Do not look forward
> To what might happen tomorrow;
> The same everlasting Father
> Who cares for you today
> Will take care of you
> Tomorrow and every day.
> Either He will shield you
> From suffering
> Or He will give you
> Unfailing strength to bear it.
> Be at peace, then, and put aside
> All anxious thoughts
> And imaginings.

*Frances de Sales*

The best thing about the future is that it comes only one day at a time.

*Abraham Lincoln*

There is little in life we have less control over than the weather. Yet have you ever found yourself worrying about the meteorological future? Probably more picnics are ruined by worry than by rain! Jesus encourages us not to worry about that which we cannot control or about that which is not important. Worry instead, He says, about your priorities and the condition of you soul. When you find yourself overcome with worry, take a careful look at the priorities of your heart. When God is firmly established at the centre of our focus and desires, worry loses its grip on our lives.

*Touchpoint – New Living Translation Bible*

*Jesus issues us with an invitation in Matthew 11. It has our name at the top and RSVP written underneath. He is challenging us to respond, and gives us the choice. We can either accept or refuse.*

'Come to Me all of you who are weary and carry heavy burdens and I will give you rest.'

## I HEARD THE VOICE OF JESUS SAY

I heard the voice of Jesus say,
'Come unto Me and rest;
Lay down, thou weary one, lay down
Thy head upon My breast':
I came to Jesus as I was,
Weary, and worn, and sad;
I found in Him a resting-place,
And He has made me glad.

I heard the voice of Jesus say,
'Behold, I freely give
The living water; thirsty one,
Stoop down, and drink, and live':
I came to Jesus, and I drank
Of that life-giving stream,
My thirst was quenched, my soul revived,
And now I live in Him.

I heard the voice of Jesus say,
'I am this dark world's light;
Look unto Me, thy morn shall rise,
And all thy day be bright':
I looked to Jesus and I found
In Him my star, my sun;
And in that light of life I'll walk
Till travelling days are done.

*Horatius Bonar*

*About a week before my husband died of cancer, he started having visions of heaven, and at one time he told me he could hear thousands of angels singing this hymn. The words could not have been more appropriate! They gave him such peace.*

## BECAUSE HE LIVES

God sent His Son, they called Him Jesus,
He came to love, heal, and forgive;
He lived and died to buy my pardon,
An empty grave is there to prove my Saviour lives.
*Because He lives I can face tomorrow;*
*Because He lives all fear is gone;*
*Because I know He holds the future,*
*And life is worth the living just because He lives.*

How sweet to hold a new-born baby,
And feel the joy and pride he gives;
But greater still the calm assurance
This child can face uncertain days because He lives.
*Because He lives I can face tomorrow ...*

And then one day I'll cross the river;
I'll fight life's final war with pain;
And then as death gives way to victory
I'll see the lights of glory and I'll know He lives.
*Because He lives I can face tomorrow ...*

*Gloria and William J. Gaither*

121

In the heart's depths a peace serene and holy
Abides, and when pain seems to have its will,
Or we despair – oh, may that peace rise slowly,
Stronger than agony, and we be still.

*Samuel Johnson*


When through fiery trials thy pathway shall lie,
His grace all-sufficient shall be thy supply,
The flame shall not hurt thee, his only design
Thy dross to consume and thy gold to refine.

The soul that on Jesus has leaned for repose
He will not, he cannot, desert to its foes;
That soul, though all hell should endeavour to shake,
He never will leave, he will never forsake.

*Richard Keen*


*The following 'rules' were written in the nineteenth century. Technology may advance and our lives become more sophisticated but human problems remain the same!*

If we wished to gain contentment, we might
try such rules as these:

1. Allow thyself to complain of nothing, not
   even of the weather.

2. Never picture thyself to thyself under any
   circumstances in which thou art not.

3.  Never compare thine own lot with that of another.

4.  Never allow thyself to dwell on the wish that this or that had been, or were, otherwise than it was, or is. God Almighty loves thee better and more wisely than thou dost thyself.

5.  Never dwell on the morrow. Remember that it is God's, not thine. The heaviest part of sorrow often is to look forward to it. 'The Lord will provide.'

*E. B. Pusey*

The little worries which we meet each day
May lie as stumbling-blocks across our way,
Or we may make them stepping-stones to be
Of grace, O Lord, to Thee.

*A. E. Hamilton*

My prayers, God, flow from what I am not;
I think thy answers make me what I am.
Like weary waves thought flows upon thought,
But the still depth beneath is all thine own,
And there thou mov'st in paths to us unknown.
Out of the strange strife thy peace is strangely
    wrought;
If the lion in us pray – thou answerest the lamb.

*George MacDonald*

123

He gives power to those who are tired and worn out; he offers strength to the weak. Even youths will become exhausted and young men will give up. But those who wait on the LORD will find new strength. They will fly high on wings like eagles. They will run and not grow weary. They will walk and not faint.

*Isaiah 40:29–31 (NLT)*

*T*he following extract is taken from Selwyn Hughes' inspiring book, The Divine Eagle:

### AN EAGLE SOARS

Isaiah says of the eagle that she 'soars' and not 'flaps'. Although, of course, an eagle is well able to use its wings to propel itself across the sky, its typical pose is that of soaring. An eagle will sometimes perch on a high rock and wait for a while – testing the winds. When it feels that the right wind is blowing, it expands its broad wings and is at once lifted by the breeze into the great heights. In every trial and difficulty that God allows to come our way, there is a breeze that, if we wait for it and take advantage of it, will lift us clean beyond the clouds where we will see the face of God.

You see, life is determined more by our reactions than our actions. When God allows things to crowd into your life, it is then that reaction counts. You can react in self-pity and frustration or with confidence and courage and turn the trouble into a triumph.

When trouble strikes and your nest is overturned – don't panic. Wait for the breeze that is springing up; it will lift you clean into the presence of God. Those that wait, that keep hoping, are those that soar. This is the eagle's secret of being able to soar so high – waiting. When troubles come, don't flap – soar!

If we are to live successfully as Christians we must come to grips with the fact that God does not permit trouble to come our way in order to destroy us but in order to develop us. When circumstances are against us, we must be able to set the tilt of our wings and use adversity to lift us higher into the presence of God.

When the storm strikes the eagle, if its wings are set in a downward tilt, it will be dashed to pieces on the ground; but if its wings are tilted upward, it will rise, making the storm bear it up beyond its fury. The Christian faith, providing we interpret it correctly and apply it to our circumstances, will set the wings of our spirit in the right direction, so that when trouble or calamity strikes, we go up and not down. The calamity that strikes one Christian finds him with his spiritual wings tilted in the direction of the earth so he writhes in anguish in the dust. The same calamity strikes another, one with his wings set upwards, and he soars above it – calm and serene.

*Here is a different illustration on the same theme by Alastair Begg from his book,* The Hand of God:

A sailor on the south coast of England told his chaplain, 'Chaplain, you don't understand. You're telling us to walk the straight and narrow path. But you don't realise the temptations we face, the way we're blown and tossed about. We can't really be blamed for what happens to us.'

The chaplain drew the sailor's attention to the water, where two sailboats were moving along with their sails flapping in the wind. One was heading west, the other east. The chaplain said, 'One boat goes east, one boat goes west. By the self-same winds that blow. It's the set of the sails and not the gales, that determine which way they go.'

Do we have our sails set in the direction of obedience to God? If so, we can go the right way, even if the whole world is blown off course. Joseph had set his sails long before Potiphar's wife tried to steer his life onto the rocks.

Leaning on Him, with reverent meekness
His own thy will,
And with strength from Him shall thy
    utter weakness
Life's task fulfil.

*J. G. Whittier*

And they that know thy name will put their
trust in thee: for thou, LORD, hast not
forsaken them that seek thee.

*Psalm 9:10 (AV)*

Some of you are perhaps feeling that you are
voyaging just now on a moonless sea.
Uncertainty surrounds you. There may seem
to be no signs to follow. Perhaps you feel
about to be engulfed by loneliness. Amy
Carmichael wrote of such a feeling when ...
she had to leave Japan because of poor
health. (This preceded her going to India,
where she stayed for fifty three years.) 'All
along, let us remember, we are not asked to
understand, but simply to obey ... We had
come on board on Friday night, and just as
the tender (a small boat) where were the dear
friends who had come to say goodbye was
moving off, and the chill of loneliness
shivered through me, like a warm love-clasp

came the long-loved lines – "And only heaven is better than to walk with Christ at midnight, over moonless seas." I couldn't feel frightened then. Praise Him for the moonless seas – all the better the opportunity for proving Him to be indeed the El-Shaddai, "the God who is Enough".'

Let me add my own word of witness to hers and to that of tens of thousands who have learned that He is indeed Enough. He is not all we would ask (if we were honest), but it is precisely when we do not have what we would ask for, and *only then*, that we can clearly perceive His all-sufficiency. It is when the sea is moonless that the Lord has become my Light.

*Elisabeth Elliot, from* Keep a Quiet Heart

Work hard for peace, even if you have to run after it to catch it and hold it.

*1 Peter 3:11 (Living Bible)*

W*ith four children that verse is not always easy to achieve, but it became very important to me to make sure there was always a happy atmosphere in my home where friends always felt welcome.*

*Many years ago I heard the Rev. David Watson speak on this verse: 'Whatever is in your heart determines what you say (Out of the heart the mouth speaks)' Luke 7:45.*
*He used the following illustration:*

*Question: 'If you are carrying a full glass and someone nudges you, what spills out?'*
*Answer: 'Whatever is in the glass'*
*Question: 'If someone nudges you, what spills out?'*
*Answer: 'Whatever is inside' (anger, bitterness, irritability? or love, joy, peace?)*

As water reflects a face, so a man's heart reflects the man.

*Proverbs 27:19 (NIV)*

I took my sketchbook and cycled down to the nature reserve near my home. It was a bright day, and a bit breezy. I stood at the edge of one of the lakes, watched the ripples on the water and tried to work out how I'd paint them.

The trouble was they kept changing colour. One moment the ripples looked sky blue, the next they were muddy brown. It's all a matter of reflection. The water's like a mirror; it reflects the blue sky when the angle's right, but when the angle changes, blown by the wind, you just see the muddy water. Both colours are true depending on your position.

In a way we all reflect what's going on around us. When life gets rough it shows in out attitudes and behaviour. It's the same with others. When someone's depressed or unresponsive maybe they're not just being bloody-minded, maybe something really is wrong and they need more understanding than we're prepared to give.

And when I find myself getting critical of other people and the way they are, perhaps if I changed my position slightly I might see them in a more favourable light. And when someone has a different point of view from mine maybe they're simply seeing things from a different angle.

*Eddie Askew, from* Slower than Butterflies

# CHAPTER TWELVE

# Take from our souls the strain and stress

\* \* \*

*I love this story by Susan Lenzkes from her delightful book,* Everybody's Breaking Pieces off of Me. *I think it's because I understand how she felt!*

Although it happened several years ago, I can still remember the feeling of the moment. It had been the kind of day when you lose track of which interruption is being interrupted. Everyone had been breaking off pieces of me, and someone had just hauled off the last scrap of this wife/mother/ friend/churchworker.

I wasn't sure what do to or where to go to find the lost pieces, but I had to do something. I stood in the family room buttoning myself into my coat.

From his observation point on the couch, my husband asked, 'And just where do you think you're going?'

With my arms slicing the air for emphasis, I announced that I didn't know and didn't care, but definitely some place remote and undemanding.

'Everybody expects too much of me!' I concluded, marching to the closet for my purse.

My husband's irritatingly calm voice followed me, 'I hope you don't plan to run too far. That car won't make it much beyond forty miles.'

Yanking off my coat, I hurled it to the floor and burst into tears. 'What am I supposed to do if I can't even run away?'

Realising that the car wouldn't make it, and neither would I, I stayed at home and began a journey that eventually led me to discover why I felt so drained, so spent, so empty. I learned that I am a helpless victim of demanding circumstances only if I *allow* myself to be!

In the midst of life's pressures, problems, and pain I am free to choose attitudes that produce stress or *reduce* it. I can *choose* to respond with humour, acceptance, and flexibility. I can act out of a sense of direction that leads to purposeful service.

These are invaluable allies in the fight to become, and remain, whole in a world that tears pieces away from our time, energy, talents and sanity.

A sense of purpose and trust in God, who knows and loves us, will help us establish priorities. Then we will learn to say 'no' without guilt and say 'yes' without reservation.

And finally we will discover the miracle of servant-living when we catch hold of the enormous truth that people *cannot take from us what we freely give away.*

This, then, is how we give ourselves away without coming apart. It is the lesson of the Cross.

The reason my Father loves me is that I lay down my life – only to take it up again. No-one takes it from me, but I lay it down of my own accord.

*John 10:17–18 (NIV)*

Your attitude should be the same as that of Christ Jesus: Who, being in very nature God, did not consider equality with God something to be grasped, but made himself nothing, taking the very nature of a servant, being made in human likeness. And being found in appearance as a man, he humbled himself and became obedient to death – even death on a cross!

*Philippians 2:5–8 (NIV)*

## STRESS

Life sometimes causes us to feel like a rubber band stretched tight. Pressures build up and pull us in different directions or pull against our sense of well being. Trying to do too much work with too little time or too few resources stretches us beyond our capacity. Trying to live in today's society with its many demands may put excessive pressures on us. Trying to cope with the financial demands of life without adequate income is a stretching experience. Marital difficulties or difficulties in parent-child relationships, or any relational difficulties can bring stress into life. What is the answer? God can bring peace in the midst of stress.

*Definition of stress from Touchpoint – New Living Translation Bible*

Peace is the result of grace. It literally means, 'To bind together.' In other words, the peace which comes from unmerited, unearned love can weave and bind our fragmented lives into wholeness. And the civil war of divergent drives, which makes us feel like rubber bands stretched in all directions, is ended. The Lord is in control. He has forgiven the past, He is in charge of now, and shows the way for each new day.

*J. Lloyd Ogilvie, found in* Let God Love You

Give all your worries and cares to God, for he cares about what happens to you.

*1 Peter 5:7 (NLT)*

Anxiety does not empty tomorrow of its sorrows, but only empties today of its strength.

*Charles Haddon Spurgeon*

Don't worry about anything; instead, pray about everything. Tell God what you need, and thank him for all he has done. If you do this, you will experience God's peace, which is far more wonderful than the human mind can understand. His peace will guard your hearts and minds as you live in Christ Jesus.

*Philippians 4:6–7 (NLT)*

We must be continually sacrificing our own wills, as opportunity serves, to the will of others; bearing, without notice, sights and sounds that annoy us; setting about this or that task, when we had far rather be doing something very different; persevering in it, often, when we are thoroughly tired of it; keeping company for duty's sake, when it would be a great joy to us to be by ourselves; besides all the trifling untoward accidents of life; bodily pain and weakness long continued, and perplexing us often when it does not amount to illness; losing what we value, missing what we desire; disappointment in other persons, wilfulness, unkindness, ingratitude, folly, in cases where we least expect it.

*John Keble*

In today's world multitudes of men and women suffer from the effects of stress. One doctor defines stress as 'the wear and tear on the personality'. Experts on stress tell us it comes from two main causes: too little change and too much change.

To function at peak efficiency we all need a certain amount of change, but when change comes too fast for us to cope with, the personality is put under tremendous pressure. Dr Thomas Holmes, a recognised authority on stress, measures it in terms of 'units of change'. The death of a loved one, for example, measures 100 units, a divorce 73 units, pregnancy 40 units, moving or refurbishing home 25 units, and Christmas is given 12 units. His conclusion is that no-one can handle more than 300 units of stress in a twelve month period without suffering physically or emotionally during the next two years.

The first thing to do when experiencing stress is to identify what is causing it. What is the trigger? Is it too little change or too much? What are the symptoms? What happened immediately prior to the symptoms occurring? (This can be a vital clue.) We must invite the Lord to help us with the matter as we think and pray it through. Only when the cause is found can things be changed.

Next, we must consider why it is that we are victims of stress. Are we unable to move ahead because of fear, or are we going too fast because we are afraid of what we might discover about ourselves if we stopped? To the degree we lack security in God, to that degree we will be motivated to find it is something else. The secure are less prone to stress because they already have what they want – peace of mind.

*Selwyn Hughes, from*
Your Personal Encourager

Father, please help me to face up to the issue
of where my true security lies – in things or
in You. For I see that the only way to live
without stress in a stressful world is to have
my inner core buttressed by You. Help me,
my Father, In Jesus' Name. Amen.

*Selwyn Hughes, from*
Your Personal Encourager

Though he slay me, yet will I trust in him.

*Job 13:15 (AV)*

There is no pit so deep that Jesus is not
deeper still.

*Corrie ten Boom*

Jesus Christ went down to the waterside, to
go in a boat, to a more retired place. And in
the boat, he fell asleep, while His disciples
were sitting on the deck. While He was still
sleeping, a violent storm arose, so that the
waves washed over the boat and the howling
wind so rocked and shook it, that they
thought it would sink. In their fright, the
disciples awoke our Saviour, and said, 'Lord!
Save us, or we are lost!' He stood up, and

raising His arm, said to the rolling sea and the whistling wind, 'Peace. Be still!'

And immediately it was calm and pleasant weather, and the boat went safely on, through the smooth waters.

*Charles Dickens*

'Don't you worry and don't you hurry.' I know that phrase by heart, and if all the other music should perish out of this world it would still sing to me.

*Mark Twain*

When I hear somebody sigh, 'Life is hard', I am always tempted to ask, 'Compared to what?'

*Sydney J. Harris*

We can rejoice, too, when we run into problems and trials, for we know they are good for us – they help us to learn to endure.

*Romans 5:3–4 (NLT)*

*The words of this hymn might be considered 'sentimental' in the twenty-first century, but I think they contain a lesson for many of us who live in this affluent society and take so much for granted. The words, when applied – work!*

## COUNT YOUR BLESSINGS, NAME THEM ONE BY ONE

When upon life's billows you are tempest tossed,
When you are discouraged, thinking all is lost,
Count your many blessings, name them one by one,
And it will surprise you what the Lord hath done.

Count your blessings, name them one by one,
Count your blessings, see what God hath done;
Count your blessings, name them one by one,
And it will surprise you what the Lord hath done.

Are you ever burdened with a load of care?
Does the cross seem heavy you are called to bear?
Count your many blessings, every doubt will fly,
And you will be singing as the days go by.

When you look at others with their lands and gold,
Think that Christ hath promised you His wealth
   untold,
Count your many blessings, money cannot buy
Your reward in heaven, nor your home on high.

So amid the conflict, whether great or small,
Do not be discouraged, God is over all,
Count your many blessings, angels will attend,
Help and comfort give you to your journey's end.

*Johnson Boatman*

Whatever the reasons for our trouble, we must not allow our souls to become so overwhelmed that we think we have committed some 'unpardonable sin'. For out of all the terror comes the soothing voice of our Lord Himself, 'Be of good cheer: it is I; be not afraid.'

Too many disciples have faith in their faith, or in their joy in the Lord; and when a spiritual storm comes, they have neither faith nor joy. Only one thing can endure, and that is love for God. If such love is not there, we will not recognise the living voice of God when He cries out to us that He is our refuge and strength, a very present help in trouble.

'... be still, and know that I am God ... ' (Psalm 46:1,10a). You are my God, and I seek strength and shelter in Your love and goodness.

*Oswald Chambers*

My heart is in anguish.
  The terror of death overpowers me.
Fear and trembling overwhelm me.
  I can't stop shaking.
Oh, how I wish I had wings like a dove;
  then I would fly away and rest!
I would fly far away
  to the quiet of the wilderness.

*Psalm 55:4–7 (NLT)*

Let us sing when we do not feel like it, for thus we may give wings to leaden feet and turn weariness into strength.

*J. A. Jowett*

*I am including the following story, which was part of a letter I recently received from my daughter who lives in Peru. It is a faith-building story of people who put their trust in the Lord, believing He hears them.*

Ruth and I have some friends who run a refuge for abandoned children here in Lima. They know a lady called Elsa who lives in a very poor area of Lima called Pachacutec. She came to Lima from the jungle to receive treatment for cancer. She is full of faith and has started a work among children in her house. She works with about 150 kids now and is also very active in the community. The other day she took a little girl who was suffering with a heart condition to hospital. She was admitted, as if she didn't have the operation she would die. However, they needed to pay 800 Soles (about £150) by six o'clock the next day, otherwise the girl would be discharged. On the way home, Elsa was encouraging the mother to have faith in God because he would provide the money. When they got off the bus, the lady who had been sitting behind them approached them and said that she had been putting aside some money to give as an offering, and had been asking God who she should give the money to, and so she gave them the money they needed for the operation.

We, as Christians, need to stop telling God how big our mountains are and start telling our mountains how big our God is.

*John Osteen*

Do not ask 'What can I do?' but 'What can he not do?'

*Corrie ten Boom*

God is our refuge and strength,
    always ready to help in times of trouble.
So we will not fear, even if earthquakes come
    and the mountains crumble into the sea.
Let the oceans roar and foam.
    Let the mountains tremble as the waters surge!

A river brings joy to the city of our God,
    the sacred home of the Most High.
God himself lives in that city; it cannot be destroyed.
    God will protect it at the break of day.
The nations are in an uproar,
    and kingdoms crumble!
God thunders,
    and the earth melts!
The Lord Almighty is here among us;
    The God of Israel is our fortress.

Come, see the glorious works of the LORD.
    See how he brings destruction upon the world
and causes wars to end throughout the earth.
    He breaks the bow and snaps the spear in two;
    he burns the shields with fire.
'Be silent and know that I am God!
    I will be honoured by every nation.
    I will be honoured throughout the world.'
The LORD Almighty is here among us;
    The God of Israel is our fortress.

*Psalm 46 (NLT)*

## FEAR

Psalm 46:1–3:
The abundance of natural disasters in recent years reminds us of the possibility of even greater disasters, such as the whole world being blown up by nuclear war! We all fear the disasters that cripple nations and societies, and leave people wounded and destitute.

The fear of atomic disaster is on the minds of many people today. *What if...?* Consider the worst disaster that could happen. Then ask yourself, 'Is God with me – or not?' Have you asked Him to be your refuge and strength? The Christian has God's assurance that, regardless of the worst, we are His forever. If the world blows apart, we will be taken immediately to be with God. For the person who remains alienated from God, such a disaster means the end of his or her chances to be reconciled and live with God forever. This is the clear teaching of the Bible.

*Touchpoint – New Living Translation Bible*

# CHAPTER THIRTEEN

# *And let our ordered lives confess*

* * *

The ultimate measure of a man is not where
he stands in moments of comfort and
convenience, but where he stands at times of
challenge and controversy.

*Martin Luther King*


IF

If you can keep your head when all about you
Are losing theirs and blaming it on you;
If you can trust yourself when all men doubt you,
But make allowance for their doubting too;
If you can wait and not be tired by waiting,
Or being lied about, don't deal in lies,
Or being hated, don't give way to hating,
And yet don't look too good, nor talk too wise;

If you can dream – and not make dreams your
    master;
If you can think – and not make thoughts your aim,
If you can meet with triumph and disaster
And treat those two impostors just the same;
If you can bear to hear the truth you've spoken
Twisted by knaves to make a trap for fools,
Or watch the things you gave your life to, broken,
And stoop and build 'em up with worn-out tools;

If you can make one heap of all your winnings
And risk it on one turn of pitch-and-toss,
And lose, and start again at your beginnings
And never breathe a word about your loss;
If you can force your heart and nerve and sinew
To serve your turn long after they are gone,
And so hold on when there is nothing in you
Except the Will which says to them: 'Hold on!'

If you can walk with crowds and keep your virtue,
Or walk with Kings – nor lose the common touch,
If neither foes nor loving friends can hurt you,
If all men count with you, but none too much;
If you can fill the unforgiving minute
With sixty seconds' worth of distance run,
Yours is the Earth and everything that's in it,
And – which is more – you'll be a Man, my son!

*Rudyard Kipling*

Our peace is refined in outwardly turbulent circumstances.

*Anon.*

In the depth of winter I finally learned that within me there lay an invincible summer.

*Albert Camus*

### GETTING RID OF FEAR

We turn our attention now to the problem of fear. The very first word of the gospel was the voice of the angel saying, 'Fear not', and the very first word of Jesus after His resurrection was, 'Have no fear'. Between the first word and the last the constant concern of Jesus was to help men and women find release from fear.

Fear has three things against it: (1) it produces sickness and disease; (2) it paralyses human effort; (3) it is counter-productive. We are made in our physical and mental make-up for faith and confidence; faith builds us up, but fear breaks us down. When God made us in the beginning He designed us to function in accordance with love, so that when love motivates our being, our bodies function in line with its destiny. When we try to make it run on any other ingredient, then it will refuse to function – and rebel. Love-deprived children grow up to be extremely fearful, because when love flows out, fear flows in.

How can we reduce fear to its proper proportion, and place this dreaded enemy of mankind in its right perspective? There is only one way. We reduce it to its proper size when we set it against the goodness and greatness of our Loving God. Set against His Almightiness, every fear is brought into perspective and shown to be the evil it is. When love flows in, fear flows out. Take a fresh look at God's unending love for you as demonstrated at Calvary, and, in the knowledge that he did all this for *you*, watch your fears melt away.

*Selwyn Hughes, from* Reflections

Courage is fear that has said its prayers.

*Anon.*

Let nothing disturb thee,
Nothing affright thee;
All things are passing:
God never changeth:
Patient endurance
Attaineth to all things:
Who God possesseth
Is nothing wanting.
Alone God sufficeth.

*St Teresa of Avila*

Do the thing you fear and the death of fear
is certain.

*Anon.*

## THE GREAT SHEPHERD

Now, may the God of peace, who brought
again from the dead our Lord Jesus, equip
you with all you need for doing his will.

*Hebrews 13:20 (NLT)*

If you are ever going to know the Shepherd's care, you must first realise your great need for a shepherd. If any animal created ever needed a shepherd, it is sheep! And I truly believe that God created sheep so that we could see what we are like.

Learning about sheep can be very humbling and very eye-opening! To learn about sheep is to see how greatly, we as sheep, need our Shepherd. It makes you cast yourself on Him in total dependence, and that is where we are meant to live!

Sheep are the dumbest of all animals. Because of this they require constant attention and meticulous care. They are helpless, timid, feeble animals that have little means of self-defence. If they do not have the constant care of a shepherd they will go the wrong way, unaware of the dangers at hand. If they are not led to proper pastures, they will obliviously eat or drink things that are disastrous to them. Not only that, but they will literally live their lives in a rut if the shepherd does not lead them to new pastures. Sheep easily fall prey to other animals, and when they do, they are virtually defenceless without their shepherd to protect them. Sheep can also become cast down and, in that state, panic and die. And so because sheep are sheep, they need shepherds to care for them.

You, beloved, are the sheep of His pasture. It was for you that God '... brought up from the dead the great Shepherd of the sheep through the blood of the eternal covenant, even Jesus our Lord' (Hebrews 13:20, NAS) and through Him, beloved, He will 'equip you in every good thing to do His will, working in us that which is pleasing in His sight ...' (Hebrews 13:21, NAS).

Oh, precious sheep take a good look at your life. How can you make it on your own? Can you see your need for a Shepherd?

*Kay Arthur, found in*
Because the Lord Is My Shepherd

When my husband died, God filled my heart with joy – not happiness – joy. It was totally unexpected, but it was overwhelming. Some months later I tried to analyse how I could have experienced such joy when my heart was breaking.

God showed me the answer through the following parable of Jesus. If my life had been based on my marriage, I might have fallen apart when my husband died, but because my life and my marriage were based on my faith in God through Jesus, that rock held me steady all through the storm.

Anyone who listens to my teaching and obeys me is wise, like a person who builds a house on solid rock. Though the rain comes in torrents and the floodwaters rise and the winds beat against the house, it won't collapse because it is built on rock. But anyone who hears my teaching and ignores it is foolish, like a person who builds a house on sand. When the rains and floods come and the winds beat against that house, it will fall with a mighty crash.

*Matthew 7:24–27 (NLT)*

Though waves and billows o'er me roll
In crushing floods of ill,
Within the haven of God's love
My soul is anchored still.

*Anon.*

Anxiety is the natural result when our hopes are centred in anything short of God and His will for us.

*Billy Graham*

In all you do, I want you to be free from worry.

*1 Corinthians 7:32 (Living Bible)*

*This beautiful song was sung at the funeral of Simon, the beloved son of the Rev. Keith and Mrs Lynne King who, as they so gently put it, was 'differently abled'. He brought so much joy into the lives of our congregation I wanted to include this, as it was one of Simon's favourites.*

## ANGELS

What a long hard day it's been
You've had to take the rough with the smooth
Those eyes are tired by what they've seen
It's not so easy standing up for truth

But forget the wars you've been in today
As nothing can disturb you now
'Cause round your bed are stationed heaven's armies
Just lay down weary child lay down
Little angel go to sleep
'Cause Father's here and He will keep you safe
'Cause Father's here and He will keep you safe

What a long hard day it's been
At times you wondered if you'd make it through
Straight and narrow's tough and mean
As the pressure really gets to you

What a long hard day it's been
To take His cross will mean you'll suffer pain
Though you're weak He'll keep you clean
Rest in Him and be renewed again.

*Ian Smale*

*A* few years ago at the Seattle Special Olympics, nine contestants, all physically or mentally disabled, assembled at the starting line for the 100-yard dash, with a relish to run the race to the finish and win.

All, that is, except one boy who stumbled on the asphalt, tumbled over a couple of times and began to cry. The other eight heard the boy cry. They slowed down and looked back. They all turned round and went back, every one of them. One girl, with Down's Syndrome, bent down and kissed him and said, 'This will make it better.' All nine linked arms and walked across the finish line together.

Everyone in the stadium stood, and the cheering went on for several minutes. People who were there are still telling the story. Why?

Because deep down we know this one thing: what matters in this life is more than winning for ourselves. What truly matters in this life is helping others win, even if it means slowing down and changing our course.

Those who live in the shelter of the Most High
   will rest in the shadow of the Almighty.
This I declare of the LORD:

He alone is my refuge, my place of safety,
    he is my God, and I am trusting him.
For he will rescue you from every trap
    and protect you from the fatal plague.
He will shield you with his wings,
    He will shelter you with his feathers.
    His faithful promises are your armour and
    protection.
Do not be afraid of the terrors of the night,
    nor fear the dangers of the day,
nor dread the plague that stalks in darkness,
    nor the disaster that strikes at midday.
Though a thousand fall at your side,
    though ten thousand are dying around you,
    these evils will not touch you.
But you will see it with your eyes;
    you will see how the wicked are punished.

If you make the LORD your refuge,
    if you make the Most High your shelter,
no evil will conquer you;
    no plague will come near your dwelling.
For he orders his angels
    to protect you wherever you go.
They will hold you up with their hands
    to keep you from striking your foot on a stone.
You will trample down lions and poisonous
    snakes;
    you will crush fierce lions and serpents under
    your feet!

The LORD says, 'I will rescue those who love me.
  I will protect those who trust in my name.
When they call on me, I will answer;
  I will be with them in trouble.
  I will rescue them and honour them.
I will satisfy them with a long life
  and give them my salvation.'

*Psalm 91 (NLT)*

## SOMETIMES

Sometimes, when the sun goes down,
It seems it will never rise again …
But it will!

Sometimes, when you feel alone,
It seems your heart will break in two …
But it won't!

And sometimes, it seems it's
Hardly worthwhile carrying on …
But it is!

*Frank Brown*

# CHAPTER FOURTEEN

# *The beauty of thy peace*

*** ***

I rest beneath the Almighty's shade,
My griefs expire, my troubles cease;
Thou, Lord, on whom my soul is stayed,
Wilt keep me still in perfect peace.

*Charles Wesley*

To some, talking about peace is a sign of cowardice – but in fact it is a sign of strength.

*Nelson Mandela*

'May the Lord of peace himself always give you his peace no matter what happens.'

*2 Thessalonians 3:16 (NLT)*

Last night I had a vivid dream ... While driving a car, I became terrified of what was ahead. With no clear idea of what the problem was, I could not seem to keep from doing the very worst thing possible – *closing my eyes as I drove.*

Then I was driving over a concrete road with about three inches of very clear water over it. There was still overwhelming fear in me. I awoke in panic.

As I pondered it this morning, the message of the dream would appear to be that my actual danger is very small – shallow water. Thus my real problem is fear itself. Fear of many things, including God himself.

He scolded me for this – gently – this morning, reminding me that fear is one of Satan's tools. The fear of God – the wrong kind, that is, fearfulness instead of awe – is something I have struggled with for so many, many years. And I sense that many believing people are like me, unable to love and praise their Heavenly Father fully because of fear – often a fear of punishment.

Then I remembered something that Jesus did. Knowing that all people struggle with fear, he often prefaced what he was about to say to his fellow humans with the words, 'Fear not.'

Therefore my prayer is, 'Lord, I hand my fears over to you, fears of all kinds. Fear of you is actually a kind of blasphemy against your character. I'm sorry. Forgive me.'

In answer to my prayer, a line from an old hymn, 'Take it to the Lord in prayer', began running through my mind. The Spirit said very clearly, 'Why do you think I am reminding you of these words? Pay attention to every line of these verses. Learn to bring everything directly to me instead of allowing so many worrying wonderings.'

*Catherine Marshall*

## WHAT A FRIEND WE HAVE IN JESUS

What a friend we have in Jesus,
All our sins and griefs to bear!
What a privilege to carry
Everything to God in prayer.
O what peace we often forfeit,
O what needless pain we bear –
All because we do not carry
Everything to God in prayer.

Have we trials and temptations?
Is there trouble anywhere?
We should never be discouraged –
Take it to the Lord in prayer.
Can we find a friend so faithful
Who will all our sorrows share?
Jesus knows our every weakness –
Take it to the Lord in prayer.

Are we weak and heavy-laden,
Cumbered with a load of care?
Precious Saviour, still our refuge –
Take it to the Lord in prayer;
Do thy friends despise, forsake thee?
Take it to the Lord in prayer;
In His arms He'll take and shield thee –
Thou wilt find a solace there.

*Joseph Scriven*

*I was profoundly moved by Sheila Walsh's book,
Honestly; therefore I was delighted to find the
following little anecdote in Barbara Johnson's
book,* God's Most Precious Jewels Are Crystallised
Tears. *'In my days of trying to be perfect,' she said,
'life had been all about me. Now ... I realised that
my life was supposed to be about others.'*

### SAY A PRAYER FOR ME

In her book, *Honestly*, she tells of a casual
encounter that reinforced the value of that
shift in attitude. She was standing at a
counter preparing to pay for something
she'd bought in a mall store, when a woman
came over to her.

'I know you must be busy and I don't
want to keep you, but I would be very
grateful if you could say a prayer for me if
God brings me to your mind,' she said.
Sheila looked into her eyes and recognised

the pained look of someone barely holding herself together. 'Do you have time for a cup of coffee?' she asked the woman.

They made their way to a coffee shop, where the woman told her about the devastating accident the week before that had killed the woman's husband and two small children. Sheila described what happened next:

'We sat there for a while holding hands, tears pouring down our cheeks. There was nothing to say, nothing that would make it better. After a while, she dried her eyes and got up to leave. We embraced and she looked deep into my eyes and thanked me. In one sense I didn't "do" anything. I didn't come up with any clever words, or magic prayers. We had just sat for a while together, two people who love God, sharing the heartbreak of life and death.

'The old Sheila would have prayed for that woman and hurried on, feeling self-satisfied that I had done a good thing. But this time I really saw her. And we touched for a moment and left, knowing our only hope is the Lord.'

*Barbara Johnson, from* God's Precious Jewels Are Crystallised Tears

For mercy has a human heart
Pity a human face
And Love, the human form divine
And Peace the human dress.

*William Blake*


## PEACE IN THE MIDST

Two painters each painted a picture to illustrate his conception of rest. The first chose for his scene, a still, lone lake among the far-off mountains.

The second threw on his canvas a thundering waterfall, with a fragile birch tree bending over the foam; and at the fork of the branch, almost wet with cataract's spray, sat a robin on its nest.

The first was only *stagnation*; the last was *rest*.

Christ's life outwardly was one of the most troubled lives that ever lived: tempest and tumult, tumult and tempest, the waves breaking over it all the time until the worn body was laid in the grave. But the inner life was a sea of glass. The great calm was always there.

At any moment you might have gone to Him and found rest. And even when the human bloodhounds were dogging Him in the streets of Jerusalem, he turned to His disciples and offered them as a last legacy, 'My peace.'

Rest is not a hallowed feeling that comes

over us in church; it is the repose of a heart
set deep in God.

*Taken from* Streams in the Desert
*by Mrs Charles E. Cowman*

May the mind of Christ my Saviour
Live in me from day to day,
By His love and power controlling
All I do and say.

May the word of God dwell richly
In my heart from hour to hour,
So that all may see I triumph
Only through His power.

May the peace of God my Father
Rule my life in everything,
That I may be calm to comfort
Sick and sorrowing.

May the love of Jesus fill me,
As the waters fill the sea;
Him exalting, self abasing,
This is victory.

May I run the race before me,
Strong and brave to face the foe,
Looking only unto Jesus,
As I onward go.

*Kate B. Wilkinson*

# CHAPTER FIFTEEN

# Breathe through the heats of our desire, thy coolness and thy balm

❋ ❋ ❋

Take delight in the LORD and he will give you your heart's desires.

*Psalm 37:4 (NLT)*

Teach us to make the most of our time, so that we may grow in wisdom.

*Psalm 90:12 (NLT)*

Yesterday is a cancelled cheque.
Tomorrow is a promissory note.
Today is cash in hand; spend it wisely.

*Anon.*

## TODAY IS ALL YOU'VE GOT

Imagine a bank which credits your account each morning with £86,400, and every evening takes back whatever you didn't use. What would you do? Draw out every penny and invest it, of course! Well, this morning God credited you with 86,400 seconds (the number in one day)! Tonight He'll write off as 'lost' what you didn't invest. You can't accumulate any of it and you can't borrow against tomorrow; you can live *only* on today's deposits. Are you getting the idea?

Make the most of this day, for the clock is running. Before you know it, you'll make *your last* withdrawal on the Bank of Time, and stand before God. David said, 'teach us to number our days aright, that we may gain a heart of wisdom' (Ps 90:12, NIV).

To realise the value of a year, ask the student who just failed an exam; or the value of a month, ask a mother who just gave birth to a premature baby; or the value of an hour, ask lovers who're just waiting to be together; or the value of a minute, ask the person who just missed a train; or the value of a second, one who just avoided an accident; or the value of a millisecond, ask the athlete who had to settle for second place in the Olympics.

Stop messing around! Get serious about

your life and your goals, and 'Make the most of every chance you get' (Eph.5:16, TM).

*Bob Gass, from* The Word for Today

No rest here below; nothing but toil and labour. And you will enjoy your rest all the more when you come to the beautiful land above. There are always trials, and tribulations, and labours here. Work on, hope on, pray on!

*D. L. Moody*

## BE A WINNER

The winner is always part of the answer,
The loser is always part of the problem.
The winner always has a programme,
The loser always has an excuse.
The winner says, 'Let me do it for you.'
The loser says, 'That is not my job.'
The winner sees an answer for every problem,
The loser sees a problem for every answer.
The winner sees a green near every sand trap,
The loser sees a sand trap near every green.
The winner says it may be difficult but it is possible,
The loser says it may be possible but it is too difficult.

*Anon.*

*It is wholly appropriate that we have desires in life, but God calls us to put him first in order that his desires for us become our desires, and not the other way round. We need to have a focus and a purpose to challenge us each day. There is always something we can do to make life a little better for others.*

Never miss an opportunity to make others
   happy;
Even if you have to leave them alone in order
   to do it.

*Anon.*

Make it a rule of life never to regret and never look back. Regret is an appalling waste of energy; you can't build on it; it is only good for wallowing in.

*Katherine Mansfield*

The impossible: What nobody can do until somebody does.

*Anon.*

To laugh is to risk appearing a fool. To weep is to risk appearing sentimental. To reach out to another is to risk involvement. To expose your feelings is to risk rejection. To place your dreams before the crowd is to risk ridicule. To love is to risk not being loved in return. To go forward in the face of overwhelming odds is to risk failure. But risks must be taken because the greatest risk of all is to risk nothing. The person who risks nothing does nothing, has nothing and is nothing. He may avoid suffering and sorrow, but he cannot learn, he cannot feel, he cannot change, he cannot grow and he cannot love. Changed by his certitudes, he is a slave. Only the person who risks is truly free.

Ask God for clarity to hear His voice, the wisdom to understand what he is saying to you, and the courage to rise up and do it!

*Bob Gass, from* The Word for Today

Excellence is the willingness to be wrong;
Perfection is being right.

Excellence is risk;
Perfection is fear.

Excellence is powerful;
Perfection is anger and frustration.

Excellence is spontaneous;
Perfection is conformity.

Excellence is accepting;
Perfection is judgement.

Excellence is giving;
Perfection is taking.

Excellence is confidence;
Perfection is doubt.

Excellence is flowing;
Perfection is pressure.

Excellence is journey;
Perfection is destination.

Excellence is surrender;
Perfection is consuming.

Excellence is trust;
Perfection is selfishness.

*Anon.*

'Whatever you can tolerate you cannot change.' When Moses saw an Egyptian beating an Israelite, anger rose up within him. His anger was a *clue*. God was calling him to change and correct it. The problem that infuriates you the most is often the one that God has assigned you to solve.

An American mother who saw her child killed by a drunken driver founded *Mothers Against Drunk Driving* (MADD). She went all the way to the White House to change the legislation and bring in mandatory prison time for repeat offenders who drive drunk. *Your passion will help you to find your life's purpose.* It was his passion for light that sustained Edison through hundreds of failed experiments and the criticism of others who had no vision of their own. It was passion to reach and change Africa with the Word of God that drove David Livingstone to go where no missionary had ever gone before.

Mother Teresa didn't just love India's starving multitude, she hated the conditions that enslave them. The strength of her purpose kept her alive in circumstances that would have killed stronger men and women. What do you love? What do you hate? Give your passion a focus! Develop it and direct it! *See it as an instruction from God. Stay in the secret place until he gives you solutions and a Holy Spirit strategy to do something about it.* Ask God to clearly show you His will for your life, today.

*Bob Gass, from* The Word for Today

Circumstances may appear to wreck our lives, and God's plans, but God is not helpless among ruins. Our broken lives are not lost or useless. God's love is still working. He comes in and takes the calamity and uses it victoriously, working out His plan of love.

*Eric Liddell*

Because the wicked refuse to do what is just, their violence boomerangs and destroys them.

*Proverbs 21:7 (NLT)*

You will keep in perfect peace all who trust in you, whose thoughts are fixed on you.

*Isaiah 26:3 (NLT)*

The particular annoyance which befell you this morning; the vexatious words which met your ear and 'grieved' your spirit; the disappointment which was his appointment for today; the slight but hindering ailment; the presence of someone who is a 'grief of mind' to you – whatever this day seemeth not joyous, but grievous, is linked in 'the good pleasure of His goodness' with a corresponding afterward of 'peaceable fruit', the very seed from which, if you only do not choke it, this shall spring and ripen.

*Frances R. Havergal*

We sleep in peace in the arms of God, when we yield ourselves up to His providence, in a delightful consciousness of His tender mercies; no more restless uncertainties, no more anxious desires, no more impatience at the place we are in; for it is God who has put us there, and who holds us in His arms. Can we be unsafe where He has placed us?

*Fénelon*

# CHAPTER SIXTEEN

# *Let sense be dumb, let flesh retire*

✳ ✳ ✳

Between 1900 and 1970, 90 million people were killed in wars; 2 trillion dollars were spent on 130 conflicts on five continents. During 1986, when there was no global war, 1.7 million dollars were spent on arms every minute.

*Anon.*

## THE ETERNAL PEACE AGREEMENT

*Recently we have had a lot of news coverage about the Northern Ireland 'Good Friday Peace Agreement'. I heard Tony Blair, the British Prime Minister, saying in effect, 'The Good Friday Peace Agreement is the best of what's on offer so we're going to stick with it.'*

*It suddenly dawned on me that his Good Friday agreement wasn't the best on offer and that if people truly believed the real Good Friday peace agreement, and lived by it, there'd be no need for wars and bombs and destruction, because Jesus' peace agreement is an eternal agreement, that puts human beings off their thrones of self-importance, greed and power and puts Jesus back in his rightful place.*

I want your will, not mine.

*Matthew 26:39 (NLT)*

War brings only suffering ... Even if we are victorious, that victory means sacrificing many people. It means their suffering. Therefore, the important thing is peace.

*Dalai Lama*

Were half the power that fills the world with terror,
Were half the wealth bestowed on camps and courts,
Given to redeem the human mind from error,
There were no need of arsenals and forts.

The warrior's name would be a name abhorr'd!
And every nation, that should lift again
Its hand against a brother, on its forehead
Would wear forevermore the curse of Cain!

Down the dark future, through long generations,
The echoing sounds grow fainter and then cease;
And like a bell, with solemn, sweet vibrations,
I hear once more the voice of Christ say, 'Peace!'

Peace! And no longer from its brazen portals
The blast of war's great organ shakes the skies!
But, beautiful as songs of the immortals,
The holy melodies of Love arise.

*Henry Wadsworth Longfellow*

*T*he following poems were written after the Omagh bombing in August 1998:

### PEACE

We need peace today,
We need peace tomorrow,
We needed peace yesterday,
But no one was around.

We got killed,
We got bombed,
We got badly injured,
But no one was around.

Peace, peace,
That's all we need.
No more bombs,
No more deaths
But no one will listen to me.

*Kirsty Guppy, aged 9*

## OUR FATHER FOR THE NATIONS

Our Father for the nations
Let Ireland rest in peace;
Hallowed be agreement
That the Troubles here must cease.
Thy Kingdom come to all of us
And give the grieving hope;
Please help this town of Omagh
In learning how to cope.
Thy will for love and unity
Be there in every heart,
To conquer the forces
That tear us apart.
Give all here the courage
To get through each day,
That the vote of Good Friday
Will be here to stay.

Your bread, may it feed us
So hearts can be strong,
And bring us together
In ending this wrong.

Forgive what I cannot;
Those men they have killed,
And left homes with space
That cannot be filled.

Take the temptation
Those bombers may face,
And replace their thinking,
With heavenly grace.

Deliver them all
From evil of mind,
And show them the love
To which they are blind.

For Thine is the Father
Who cares for this isle,
And carries our cross
Through each difficult mile.

Your power and glory
Will bring to an end.
The decades of heartache
So little can mend.

Forever and ever
This country will stand,
Asking your blessing
Of peace on this land.
Amen.

*Joanna Grant*

Beside the site devastated by Saturday's hellfire blast, the two rivers that wash and soothe our town flow into each other and travel on together to the distant sea. They have always been a symbol of who we are here: two but one, Catholic-Protestant, unionist-nationalist; we need each other to make each other, we accept each other's differences and together welcome all others who blend with us.

We will not change though so many dear hearts have ceased to beat. Their blood has flowed together at the bottom of our street. We who must bury them now will walk together to their too-early graves and together into the future.

*Fr Kevin Mullan, Omagh, 17 August 1998*

There is a time for everything, and a season for every activity under heaven ... a time for war and a time for peace.

*Ecclesiastes 3:1, 8 (NIV)*

O God of love, O King of peace,
Make wars throughout the world to cease;
The wrath of sinful man restrain:
Give peace, O God, give peace again.

Remember, Lord, thy works of old,
The wonders that our fathers told;
Remember not our sin's dark stain:
Give peace, O God, give peace again.

Whom shall we trust but thee, O Lord?
Where rest but on thy faithful word?
None ever called on thee in vain:
Give peace, O God, give peace again.

Where saints and angels dwell above,
All hearts are knit in holy love;
O bind us in that heavenly chain:
Give peace, O God, give peace again.

*H. W. Baker*

Wilfred Owen described himself as 'a conscientious objector with a very seared conscience'. He had come to see war as absolutely evil in the agonies and senseless waste it caused; on the other hand, only as a combatant could he conscientiously and effectively speak for the men who were suffering from it. This conflict within himself was a basic motive of his war poems, of which I have included two. He was killed in action in 1918.

## ANTHEM FOR DOOMED YOUTH

What passing-bells for these who die as cattle?
Only the monstrous anger of the guns.
Only the stuttering rifles' rapid rattle
Can patter out their hasty orisons.
No mockeries now for them; no prayers nor bells,
Nor any voice of mourning save the choirs –
The shrill, demented choirs of wailing shells;
And bugles calling for them from sad shires.

What candles may be held to speed them all?
Not in the hands of boys, but in their eyes
Shall shine the holy glimmers of good-byes.
The pallor of girls' brows shall be their pall;
Their flowers the tenderness of patient minds,
And each slow dusk a drawing-down of blinds.

*Wilfred Owen*

## THE SEND-OFF

Down the close, darkening lanes they sang their way
To the siding-shed,
And lined the train with faces grimly gay.

Their breasts were stuck all white with wreath and
    spray
As men's are, dead.

Dull porters watched them, and a casual tramp
Stood staring hard,
Sorry to miss them from the upland camp.
Then, unmoved, signals nodded, and a lamp
Winked to the guard.

So secretly, like wrongs hushed-up, they went.
They were not ours:
We never heard to which front these were sent.

Nor there if they yet mock what women meant
Who gave them flowers.

Shall they return to beatings of great bells
In wild train-loads?
A few, a few, too few for drums and yells,
May creep back, silent, to still village wells
Up half-known roads.

*Wilfred Owen*

Why do the nations rage?
　　Why do the people waste their time with
　　futile plans?
The kings of the earth prepare for battle;
　　the rulers plot together
against the Lord
　　and against his anointed one.

*Psalm 2:1, 2 (NLT)*

Returning hate for hate multiplies hate, adding deeper darkness to a night already devoid of stars. Darkness cannot drive out darkness; only light can do that. Hate cannot drive out hate; only love can do that. Hate multiplies hate, violence multiplies violence, and toughness multiplies toughness in a descending spiral of destruction. So when Jesus says 'Love your enemies', he is setting forth a profound and ultimately inescapable admonition. Have we not come to such an impasse in the modern world that we must love our enemies – or else? The chain reaction of evil – hate begetting hate, wars producing more wars – must be broken, or we shall be plunged into the dark abyss of annihilation.

*Martin Luther King*

Lord, remember not only the men and women of good will but also those of ill will. But do not only remember the suffering they have inflicted on us; remember the fruits we have brought, thanks to this suffering – our comradeship, our loyalty, our humility, the courage, the generosity, the greatness of heart which has grown out of all this, and when they come to judgment, let all the fruits we have borne be their forgiveness.

*Prayer found at Ravensbruck*
*concentration camp*

I thanked God for my experiences in the concentration camp. Now I could tell these people about my experience of the reality of Jesus Christ in the hell of Ravensbruck. The fact that I also had suffered aroused their interest, and I was entitled to speak, because I could understand them.

*Corrie ten Boom*

You are my hiding place;
　　you protect me from trouble.
　　You surround me with songs of victory.

*Psalm 32:7 (NLT)*

Ah! When shall all men's good
Be each man's rule, and universal peace
Lie like a shaft of light across the land?

*Alfred, Lord Tennyson*

There can be no peace as long as there is
grinding poverty, social injustice, inequality,
oppression, environmental degradation and
as long as the weak and small continue to be
down-trodden by the mighty and powerful.

*Dalai Lama*

Pain insists on being attended to. God
whispers to us in our pleasures, speaks in our
conscience, and shouts in our pain. It is His
megaphone to rouse a deaf world.

*C. S. Lewis*

## VALLEY OF THE SHADOW

God, I am travelling out to death's sea,
I, who exulted in sunshine and laughter,
Dreamed not of dying – death is such waste of me! –
Grant me one prayer: Doom not the hereafter
Of mankind to war, as though I had died not –
I, who in battle, my comrade's arm linking,
Shouted and sang, life in my pulses hot
Throbbing and dancing! Let not my sinking
In dark be for naught, my death a vain thing!
God, let me know it the end of man's fever!
Make my last breath a bugle call, carrying
Peace o'er the valleys and cold hills forever!

*John Galsworthy*

'Don't be afraid, for I am with you. Do not
be dismayed, for I am your God. I will
strengthen you. I will help you. I will uphold
you with my victorious right hand.'

*Isaiah 41:10 (NLT)*

## PEACE

My soul, there is a country
Far beyond the stars,
Where stands a wingèd sentry
All skilful in the wars;
There, above noise and danger,
Sweet Peace sits crown'd with smiles,
And One born in a manger
Commands the beauteous files.
He is thy gracious Friend,
And – O my soul, awake! –
Did in pure love descend
To die here for thy sake.
If thou can'st get but thither,
There grows the flower of Peace,
The Rose that cannot wither,
Thy fortress, and thy ease.
Leave then thy foolish ranges,
For none can thee secure,
But one who never changes –
Thy God, thy life, thy cure.

*Henry Vaughan*

Beauty for brokenness. Hope for despair,
Lord, in the suffering this is our prayer.
Bread for the children, justice, joy, peace,
Sunrise to sunset your kingdom increase.

God of the poor, Friend of the weak
Give us compassion we pray
Melt our cold hearts, let tears fall like rain
Come change our love from a spark to a flame.

Shelter for fragile lives, cures for their ills
Work for the craftsmen, trade for their skills,
Land for the dispossessed, might for the weak
Voices to plead the cause of those who can't speak.

Refuge from cruel wars, havens from fear
Cities for sanctuary, freedoms to share
Peace to the killing fields, scorched earth to green
Christ for the bitterness, His cross for the pain.

Rest for the ravaged earth, oceans and streams.
Plundered and poisoned, our future, our dreams.
Lord, end our madness, carelessness, greed;
Make us content with the things that we need.

Lighten our darkness, breathe on this flame,
Until Your justice, burns brightly again;
Until the nations learn of your ways,
Seek You salvation and bring You their praise.

*Graham Kendrick*

Lead me from death to life
From falsehood to truth
Lead me from despair to hope
From fear to trust
Lead me from hate to love
From war to peace
Let peace fill our hearts
Our world our universe.

*Anon.*

# CHAPTER SEVENTEEN

# *Speak through the earthquake, wind and fire*

❋ ❋ ❋

*T*he hymnwriter here refers to the story of Elijah, who heard God, not in the fearsome noise of earthquake and wind, or the fury of the fire, but in the quiet gentle whisper that can only be heard in the stillness. I Kings 19:11–12 says:

'Go out and stand before me on the mountain,' the LORD told him. And as Elijah stood there, the LORD passed by, and a mighty windstorm hit the mountain. It was such a terrible blast that the rocks were torn loose, but the LORD was not in the wind. After the wind there was an earthquake but the LORD was not in the earthquake. And after the earthquake there was a fire, but the LORD was not in the fire. And after the fire there was the sound of a gentle whisper.

*1 Kings 19:11–12 (NLT)*

There is a voice, a 'still, small voice' of love,
Heard from above;
But not amidst the din of earthly sounds,
Which here confounds;
By those withdrawn apart it best us heard,
And peace, sweet peace, breathes in each
    gentle word.

*Anon.*

*It is possible to hear from God through quiet meditation of the Scriptures.*

All Scripture is inspired by God and is useful to teach us what is true and to make us realise what is wrong in our lives. It straightens us out and teaches us to what is right. It is God's way of preparing us in every way, fully equipped for every good thing God wants us to do.

*2 Timothy 3:16–17 (NLT)*

He speaketh, but it is with us to hearken or no. It is much, yea, it is everything, not to turn away the ear, to be willing to hearken, not to drown His voice. 'The secret of the Lord is with them that fear Him.' It is a secret, hushed voice, a gentle intercourse of heart to heart, a still, small voice, whispering to the inner ear. How should we hear it, if we fill our ears and our hearts, with the din of this world, its empty tumult, its excitement, its fretting vanities, or cares, or passions, or anxieties, or show, or rivalries, and its whirl of emptinesses?

*E. B. Pusey*

'My thoughts are completely different from yours,' says the LORD. 'And my ways are far beyond anything you could imagine. For just as the heavens are higher than the earth, so are my ways higher than your ways, and my thoughts higher that your thoughts.'

*Isaiah 55: 8, 9 (NLT)*

*No matter how long I live and how hard I study, I will never understand why God chose to send Jesus, why he had to die and why his death paid for my sins. I believe it because my life changed immeasurably the day I took that leap of faith from despair to trust, from fear to peace. I simply have to accept, with my poor mind, that it is a mystery, and know, like Peter, that I have no one else to whom I could go.*

At this point many of his disciples turned away and deserted Him. Then Jesus turned to the Twelve and asked, 'Are you going to leave too?'

Simon Peter replied, 'Lord, to whom would we go? You alone have the words that give eternal life. We believe them and we know You are the Holy One of God.'

*John 6:66–69 (NLT)*

And can it be that I should gain
An interest in the Saviour's blood?
Died He for me who caused His pain?
For me, who Him to death pursued?
Amazing love! How can it be
That Thou, my God shouldst die for me?

'Tis mystery all! ...

*Charles Wesley*

Next to the might of God, the serene beauty of a holy life is the most powerful influence for good in all the world.

*D. L. Moody*

# CHAPTER EIGHTEEN

# *O still small voice of calm!*

\* \* \*

Be still my soul: thy God doth undertake
To guide the future as He has the past.
Thy hope, Thy confidence let nothing shake;
All now mysterious shall be bright at last.

*Katherina Von Sheghl*

I look not back: God knows the fruitless efforts,
The wasted hours, the sinning and regrets:
I leave them all with Him who blots the record,
And graciously forgives and then forgets.

I look not forward, God sees all the future,
The road that long, or short, will lead me home.
And He will face me with each trial
And bear with me the burden that may come.

But I look up, up to the face of Jesus:
For there my heart can rest, my fears are stilled
And there is joy and love and light for darkness
And perfect peace and every hope fulfilled.

*Anon., sent to the charity Through the Roof*

Let us strip off every weight that slows us
down, especially the sin that so easily hinders
our progress. And let us run with patience
the race that God has set before us.

*Hebrews 12:1 (NLT)*

God of ancient calm, let your peace still us:
God of fearful storm, fill us with your awe:
God of the lonely plains, touch the empty spaces
Within us,
Where we are vulnerable enough
To meet you.

*Anon.*

*The man who knows right from wrong and has good judgement and common sense is happier than the man who is immensely rich!*
Whoever finds me finds life.
The Lord says: Let the wise man not bask in his wisdom, nor the mighty man in his might, nor the rich man in his riches. Let them boast in this alone: That they truly know me, and understand that I am the Lord of justice and of righteousness whose love is steadfast; And that I love to be this way. *The reverence and fear of God are basic to all wisdom.*
But all these things I once thought very worthwhile – now I've thrown them all away so that I can put my trust and hope in Christ alone. Yes, everything else is worthless when compared with the priceless gain of knowing Christ Jesus my Lord. I have put aside all else, counting it worth less than nothing, in order that I can have Christ.

In him lie all the mighty, untapped treasures of wisdom and knowledge.

I, Wisdom, give good advice and common sense. Because of my strength, kings reign in power.

Christ Jesus ... showed us God's plan of salvation; he was the one who made us acceptable to God; he made us pure and holy and gave himself to purchase our salvation.

All who win souls are wise.

*From* Living Light

## TAKE MY LIFE AND LET IT BE

Take my life, and let it be
Consecrated, Lord, to thee;
Take my moments, and my days,
Let them flow in ceaseless praise.

Take my hands, and let them move
At the impulse of Thy love;
Take my feet, and let them be
Swift and beautiful for thee.

Take my voice, and let me sing
Always, only for my King;
Take my lips, and let them be
Filled with messages from thee.

Take my silver and my gold,
Not a mite would I withhold;
Take my intellect, and use
Every power as thou shalt choose.

Take my will, and make it thine;
It shall be no longer mine;
Take my heart, it is thine own;
It shall be thy royal throne.

Take my love; my Lord, I pour
At thy feet its treasure store:
Take myself, and I will be
Ever, only, all, for thee.

*Frances R. Havergal*

If you take the gift of God you are saved. If
you have eternal life you need not fear fire,
death, or sickness. Let disease or death
come, you can shout triumphantly over the
grave if you have Christ.
My friends, what are you going to do with
Him?
Will you not decide now?

*D. L. Moody*

And let the peace that comes from Christ
rule in your hearts.

*Colossians 3:15 (NLT)*

May the LORD bless you
　and protect you
May the LORD smile on you
　and be gracious to you
May the LORD show you his favour
　and give you his peace.

*Numbers 6:24–26 (NLT)*

# Index of first lines, titles and authors

\*\*\*

·